ONTO CENTER STAGE | THE BIBLICAL WOMAN

Cherry
Orchard
Books

ONTO CENTER STAGE

THE BIBLICAL WOMAN

SARA REGUER

BOSTON
2022

Library of Congress Control Number: 2022937200

ISBN 9781644698907 (hardback)
ISBN 9781644698914 (paperback)
ISBN 9781644698921 (adobe PDF ebook)
ISBN 9781644698938 (ePub)

Copyright © 2022, Academic Studies Press
All rights reserved.

Book design by Tatiana Vernikov
Cover design by Ivan Grave
On the cover: "Chamber Music, 2022" by Raffaele Fodde and fragments of the following works—"Judith," by Giorgione, "Rebecca the Girl from Judea," by Charles H. Rolt, "Ruth," by Alexandre Cabanel, "Sara," by Jan Saenredam, "Debora and Barak," by Salomon de Bray, "Queen Esther," by Edwin Long.

Published by Cherry Orchard Books, an imprint of Academic Studies Press
1577 Beacon Street
Brookline, MA 02446, USA
press@academicstudiespress.com
www.academicstudiespress.com

"... Rabbenu Shlomo, my mother's father [i.e., **RASHI**] ... was careful to explain [**the Biblical text**], but I, Shmuel [**RASHBAM**] argued with him, and he informed me that if he had the time he would rework his commentaries according to literal sense [**PSHAT** and not exegesis/**midrash**]."

—RASHBAM, Genesis 37:1.

RASHI—Rabbi Shlomo Yitzchaki, 1040–1105 CE.
RASHBAM—Rabbi Shmuel ben Meir, c.1085–c. 1158 CE.

Contents

Introduction	IX
Sara	1
Rebecca	21
Rahel and Leah	39
Powerless Women: Dina and Tamar	57
Miriam and Tzippora: Sisters-in-Law	73
Deborah the Judge	87
Ruth	99
Chana	115
David's Wives: Michal, Avigayil, Bathsheba	131
Esther	157
Addendum: Reclaiming the Heroic Jewish Judith	173

Introduction

The Biblical narrative is usually very terse and often cryptic. Over the millennia, Jewish scholars have tried to read between the lines of the text, using their creative imaginations to fill in the missing details. Some of their musings and opinions were recorded in a variety of places, but it was the early medievalist known by the acronym RASHI (Rabbi Shomo Yitzchaki) who wrote many of these *midreshei aggada* (textual interpretations) down in an organized fashion. In the centuries following this, and especially after the invention of printing, all Jewish children learned Bible with Rashi, to the point that the text and the *midrash* almost merged into one.

When I was young, I loved these *midrashim*, but as I matured, I was annoyed by some of them. Nowadays there is a term to describe them that explains my annoyance: patriarchal. For example, when the angels visit Abraham after he circumcised himself to inform him of the impending destruction of Sodom and Gomorrah, as well as predicting the birth of Isaac, they ask him, "Where is Sara?" and Abraham responds, "In the tent." The *midrash* adds "Out of modesty." So women only belong inside, protected, private? They are not to take on public roles of leadership? Everything is written from a male point of view and with an agenda, in this case formulating the Diaspora roles for women as family-centered only. The decision to relegate specific roles to men and women was unofficially taken as a way for a minority religious community scattered all over the world to survive over the centuries. Any woman who stepped out of these post-Biblical roles was to be explained away. Thus, there are even some distinctly anti-women comments. For example, when Deborah is introduced in the text as "Deborah, wife of Lapidot," the *midrash* adds: "She was chosen because of her husband's good reputation." Really? All my students know by this time to respond in class: "So why wasn't he chosen, but she was?" Could it be that the men in the post-Biblical period couldn't deal with women leaders and therefore came up with this way of demeaning women's public roles?

Not only that, but as my education into Middle Eastern studies deepened, I also realized that there were errors, that the writers did not know the history of ancient times. One of my teachers—Dr. Nechama Leibovitz—gave me sage advice: "When it comes to a Rashi *midrash*, do not focus on the *midrash*, but ask yourself—What is bothering Rashi? Why is he focusing on this word or that word?" That advice clicked in my brain. So when I created my course on "The Jewish Woman" at Brooklyn College and prepared to teach the first section, on the Biblical woman, I began with questioning the text. Using my knowledge of the ancient Middle East, as well as my practical approach to reality, I developed my own method of reading between the lines. Over the years I have refined my approach, and it always satisfies me when I see the looks on some of my students" faces—brought up on text/Rashi—as the light dawns on them that there can be a woman's interpretation of the narrative.

The Biblical narrative is not only important to Jews, but also to Christians, and is part of Western civilization. In this case, the narrative focuses on the women who became the role models for women over the millennia. Yes, these women should be role models, but not as interpreted by men. They should be role models as they really were in real time, and in the context of an ancient society. In other words, it has been a couple of centuries since the ghetto walls of the Jews were thrown down and Jews became citizens in their modernizing countries. It is time for the final walls to be thrown down, namely the walls built up to "protect" the Jewish woman.

The curtain rises on the Biblical woman and we see her mainly in the roles she plays within the family structure. The ancient Middle Eastern family structure is a complicated one. It is patriarchal, with the oldest male at the head, making all decisions, and with power over life and death. It is patrilocal: a young woman who gets marries moves into her

Introduction

husband's family household. It is also patrilineal, with the lineage of very few women recorded.

Polygyny is a key descriptive term for this ancient family. Depending on the wealth of the patriarch, he could have numerous primary wives—each with specific matriarchal powers—as well as secondary wives, whose children's status depended on the actions of the patriarch. A further complication in the women's world was the existence of concubines, usually slave women whose children were also slaves.

This was an endogamous family, usually with cousins marrying cousins, thereby keeping the wealth within the family, as every marriage involved the payment of brideswealth (e.g., Rebecca, Rahel, Leah). A young woman therefore moved into her husband's compound and came under the rule of her mother-in-law, who was often her aunt. Thus she would be protected. She rarely became a matriarch, in charge of the women's world, until many years passed. The family was an extended family, with at least three generations living together. Not only were there grandparents and grandchildren, but there were also divorced women who returned to their father's or brother's home. Brothers were always there to protect their sisters.

A final element of this ancient family were the slaves. Depending on the wealth of the family, slaves would be used in the fields, tending the flocks, and doing heavy household chores. Talented slaves could rise to positions of power—e.g. Eliezer, Abraham's slave—but most were anonymous laborers.

Our information comes from Bible scholarship, literature, anthropology, ethnography, history, archaeology, and material culture. But the main primary source of women's lives is the Bible itself, read within the context of historical reality, and not as interpreted by writers living thousands of years after the fact.

The ancient Middle East is the world of Sumer, Chaldea, Akkadia, Pharaonic Egypt; the land of the Hittites, the land of the Philistines, Sab'a (Sheba); the land of the nomads of Arabia, Phoenicia, Persia, and the city-states of Canaan. The Hebrews—also known as the Israelites—were very much part of this world with one major exception: they were monotheists. The Biblical narrative reflects this reality and therefore has to be read in this context.

An example of how ancient Middle Eastern society is reflected in the Bible is what was considered accepted behavior. For example, nomads had to be invited by a city-state to settle in the area, for this included sharing water (see Abraham, Isaac). It was accepted behavior that women at the lower rungs of the family could not approach a patriarch (Tamar). It was accepted that rape brought group dishonor and shame, which could lead to group revenge (Dina). Honor killings are still part of Middle Eastern culture.

As for laws that became very much part of Israelite life, there is levirate marriage, which occurred when a man died leaving a childless widow. She had no choice but to cohabit with her brother-in-law and the first child born would be the spiritual heir of the dead man (see Tamar, Ruth).

Widows could not inherit the property of their dead husbands (Naomi, Ruth). However, they had a lien on the property which had to be redeemed by the dead man's closest male relative. The funds from this would support the widow until she remarried or died.

Matriarchal powers are also reflected in the text. The primary wife had total control of the women's world (Sara). If there was more than one primary wife, they determined with whom the patriarch would co-habit, as sex was one of their rights (Rahel, Leah). The primary wife could also adopt a slave's child (Rahel, Leah). Her power was sometimes manifested through the act of naming a child. An upper-class primary wife was protected through an actual written contract which gave her the right, among other things, to refuse to allow the patriarch to marry another woman (probably the reference of Ploni Almoni in the Scroll of Ruth). This was done to protect her children's inheritance.

When the monarchy begins in ancient Israel, it starts out on a modest level. This changes when David takes over and builds a palace in Jerusalem. His wives compete with each other as do his sons, and the atmosphere is anything but peaceful. The most powerful woman was the *Gevira*, or mother of the crown prince, but she—as in the case Bathsheba—had to be constantly on guard to protect her son, even after he became king.

Introduction

The world of the Persian court is totally alien to the ancient Jews, and the story of Esther is unique and distinct in Biblical history. Interestingly, over the millennia, we hear echoes of other Jewish women, who through their roles as mistresses of non-Jewish rulers were able to act to save their people in times of peril. This is not a preferred role model for a Jewish woman, but is thrust upon her from outside.

Personally I prefer the heroic Judith, which is why I have reprinted the chapter that I wrote on her as an addendum to this book. This chapter summarizes my analysis of why Judith almost disappeared from Jewish tradition.

The fictional narrative is mine alone. It is used as a tool to bring the Biblical woman from the sidelines onto center stage. It is as valid an interpretation as the creative *midrashim* of the past that tried to keep women on the sidelines because the writers" attitudes reflected their own time period and Jewish reality rather than the historic reality of the ancient world.

This is not the place for Biblical analysis, but for those interested, a good starting point would be John H. Walton, *Ancient Israelite Literature in its Cultural Context: A Survey of Parallels Between Biblical and Ancient Near Eastern Texts* (Zonderva, 1990) and Robert Alter, *The Art of Biblical Narrative* (Basic Books, 1981).

I dedicate this book to the four decades of students at Brooklyn College who took my class on "The Jewish Woman." I include my students from the Istituto Orientale of the University of Naples, where I was invited to be a visiting professor specifically lecturing on "The Biblical Woman."

Sara

The curtain rises on the Biblical woman in history with the appearance of Sarai, the first Matriarch. Unlike the women who are in Genesis before her appearance on the scene, Sara is real and fleshed out. The first woman, Eve, does not live in a historical setting, and other women mentioned in passing, such as Noah's wife, are mere shadows. In stark contrast to this, Sarai lives in the full light of history, and we may make intelligent comments about what her early life was like even if the Bible doesn't spell out the details.

Sarai was born and raised in a great center of ancient civilization, Ur of the Chaldees, located in the south of modern Iraq. Her family was comfortable, and she had all the things a girl of her class would have while growing up. The center of her life was the women's quarter of her house, where she would share her mother's rooms and play with her full and half-siblings. While the boys would gradually move out into the more public parts of the household, she and her sisters would remain mainly in the women's sector. There she would learn how to perform the basic tasks that all women learned: food preparation, weaving, spinning, washing, cleaning. Although Sarai's family would have slaves to perform the menial tasks, she would have to learn how to do them in order to be able to supervise properly.

Sarai would have a number of robes to wear, her most luxurious ones saved for special occasions. The style was approximately the same for each; it was the fabric that determined the luxuriousness of the robe. Sarai probably had at least one robe made of the finest Egyptian linen for the summer as well as one made of the softest lambswool for the winter. She would wear her hair long and braided, to be covered each time she went outside to protect it from the dust that was everywhere in Ur. She had little pots of perfumed oils as she got older, and her parents probably gave her thin dangling gold earrings as well as brightly colored necklaces and bracelets. She had a selection of leather sandals to wear as well, heavy ones for walking through the by-ways of Ur, and delicate ones for wearing indoors.

At the age of twelve, Sarai's marriage was arranged by her father and her future father-in-law. She had no official say in the matter; neither did her future husband. But no one dreamed of objecting, for this was just the way things were.

As was usual, her betrothed was a close relative. Preferred marriages were with first cousins, or in this case her betrothed was possibly a half-brother, for it was not considered wrong to marry someone who had the same father as you did but not the same mother. In any case, Abram was certainly a close relative, and this ensured that Sarai would remain on the same social status that she had been born into, and that the wealth that had to be paid by the groom's side of the family to the bride's side remained in the family. This "mohar," or bridesealth, would be Sarai's insurance to protect her in case of the death of her husband or divorce by him. It took the form of silver and gold and other valuables, as befitting a wealthy upper class urban family. She also would receive jewelry from her own father that would remain hers even after the marriage.

Abram was not a stranger to her, and she probably had known from early childhood that she would be marrying him even though, as children, a ten-year difference must have seemed enormous. Yet, when she reached the age of fourteen, suddenly twenty-four did not seem so huge an age difference anymore, and this shrank even more as she reached twenty-four herself.

Another positive aspect to marrying her cousin was that her move to her mother-in-law's domain was not a shock, for her mother-in-law was probably her aunt (or her mother's co-wife). Sarai would feel sorry for the bride brought in from outside the family, for there was no one to protect her and she would feel alone.

There were about six months for Sarai to prepare for her wedding. During this time, she had to attend to a long list of specific preparations of new household goods as well as personal clothing. She would spend much time with her mother choosing and ordering carpets, mats, pottery, cooking utensils of the latest styles from faraway places like Scythia.

Fabrics were discussed, colors decided upon, expensive threads debated over, designs for embroidery worked on, leaf shaped gold necklaces bought, silver headpieces to be worked in scarves ordered. Pillow covers were left to the slaves to weave and then stuff with the softest sheep fleeces. Makeup like kohl imported from Egypt in tiny glass pots was bought in a special part of the market, along with the vermillion for lips and the balm from Canaan. Her mother, while showing Sarai how to take care of these grown-up things, also explained to her women's lore of love and life. Even though her daughter would be moving away from her immediate care, she would still be there for visits. Little did her mother know just how far Sarai would be moving from Ur.

The day of the wedding finally arrived. Sarai was excited and nervous at the same time, but as a young woman of high status she could not let her nervousness show. What would all those silly giggling slaves do if they knew how strange she felt. She was bathed and oiled; her hair had taken hours to prepare, with all of the tiny braids elaborately worked into the latest hair style. He body hair had been removed with depilatories and the palms of her hands and feet had been dyed with red henna. The dress, so fussed over, was a masterpiece of red-purple tissue-thin wool shot through with gold thread, embroidered along the hem and the neck. Her father's gift of the leaf-shaped gold necklace was hooked into place, along with the matching dangling gold earrings. On her arms were Abram's betrothal gifts, wide gold bracelets encrusted with turquoise. Her sandals had gold leaf worked into them and a piece of matching wool fabric cleverly entwined in the ties. Her mother's gift of the tooled gold nose ring was in place, and her mother added a final touch of precious perfume from a vial so tiny it was worn as a neck adornment. Sarai examined herself in the copper mirror one last time as she heard the sounds of the hired musicians playing the flute, lyre, and small drum nearing.

She was escorted from the women's quarters by the older women into the open public space of the household off which all the other rooms opened. She saw her father smiling proudly, next to him, looking as nervous as she felt, was her betrothed, looking most handsome in his new robe, beard trimmed in the latest Ur fashion. Her father came forward, took her hand and escorted her to her new husband. The contract for her marriage had already been signed and notarized, for upper class women were protected in this way. Sarai had read the contract herself as the scribe had written it in his cuneiform script; her father had indulged her by having her educated when he saw how quick she was to learn the alphabet. Why not, he felt, one more pair of trustworthy eyes to help him with his accounts.

The temple priest was there to bless the occasion, but Abram didn't want him there. He had already told Sarai of his incredible new ideas about the gods and the One. She had thought hard about his confidences and found that they made sense. So the temple priest was just indulged in briefly, more for the sake of the company, and she sat with the women for the feast of celebration, while Abram sat with the men. The food was abundant—roast lamb, kid and antelope, fresh fish from the river, vegetables, grains—and the wine flowed; fresh fruit was brought in along with the pièce de résistance, almonds dipped in honey and rolled in dates. The musicians played, the performing dancers entertained the guests, and then to the cheers of the celebrants, the groom led the bride into their new quarters to consummate the marriage.

Seven days of celebrations and feasting followed, ensuring that all the family members and business acquaintances, and men of power with their wives, were entertained. Finally the bride and groom could peacefully start to build their relationship. From the very beginning Sarai knew that her husband was different, for he talked to her. Other women spoke of how their husbands only needed them to prepare the food and supervise their comforts; they did not treat them any better than the slaves in other respects, although they indulged them with gifts at the time of childbirth. Abram, however, talked with her, discussing everything from business to local politics, to his as yet amorphous ideas about the Divine. She responded to this attention and flourished, while carefully marking the line between the women's world and that of the men. She came under her mother-in-law's domain and had to make sure that she behaved properly, as the newest and youngest member of the women's household. But as a free woman she was superior to all the slaves and even to the concubines of her father-in-law. The pecking order was strictly adhered to, but in the privacy of their two-room apartment, off the main courtyard, Sarai and Abram began to develop a unique marital relationship.

Time passed, but the expected did not happen. The household whispered about the lack of the arrival of a child. After a few years, Abram's father tactfully suggested a second wife. Sarai held her head high, but was getting more upset as each month passed, and the childless years followed one another. Before anything could happen, Abram received his calling: he was told by his God to set out from Ur for the land of Canaan. Sarai wholeheartedly agreed, for in addition to being a believer in her husband's destiny, she welcomed a way to get away from the gossiping extended household and become the head of her own home. Who knew? A change of climate might even reverse her childlessness.

Sarai may have been disappointed to discover that she and Abram would not be leaving alone, but her father-in-law and his wives, a son and grandson with their wives, would also be leaving Ur. Then the excitement involved in selling the properties and businesses and large pieces of household goods took over. The family was moving into the sheep-raising business with a sideline in goats. Healthy animals had to be purchased along with slaves experienced in animal husbandry. The rest of the wealth was converted into easily transportable silver as well as goods that could be traded. The camels had to be loaded with household items and tents acquired for the long trip. Food and water appropriate for the long desert route were purchased at the last minute, as the caravan got underway heading north-by-northwest along the Fertile Crescent "king's way."

Sarai had packed her own household's possessions, giving away things that she no longer felt were needed. But although she knew that she would never be a big city woman again, she kept a few pairs of delicate sandals and carefully packed away her perfumes and creams. She would ride the camels but would also walk along with the animals, getting dusty and thirsty. The freedom of the trip, out of the cloistered existence of city women, was so exhilarating. Camping out each evening, while preparing the simple meals, brought back the reality of not yet being free of her mother-in-law's supervision, but Sarai knew that this was soon to come to an end. From all the complaining around her, she knew that at the first major city they reached, which would probably be Haran, her father-in-law's family would settle down. That would leave Abram free to move on to Canaan. And that was what happened. The only unforeseen event was the choice of Lot, Abram's fatherless nephew, to go to Canaan with them. Sarai did not like Lot, if only because she could see that the real reason for accompanying his uncle was not love nor belief in Abram's God, but the desire to inherit Abram's vast wealth, for Sarai was still childless.

Her father-in-law and family remained in Haran, leaving Abram and Sarai to continue on the road to Canaan. She was now the matriarch of her own household, in charge of all the women and all the women's work. She had many years of experience, under both her mother's supervision and then her mother-in-law's, to know just what to do. She was firm yet fair, and everyone knew their place in the household pecking order. When anyone stepped out of line, Sarai would discreetly remind them of their role in the huge extended family.

Canaan was beautiful but harsh. The semi-nomadic life satisfied Sarai. Occasionally she daydreamed about the luxurious bath houses of Ur, but otherwise the freedom was worth everything. She watched as her husband grew stronger in his relationship with his God, a bit jealous because for her it was a second-hand experience, but his excitement and faith were contagious.

Then the rains didn't arrive on time. The wells did not supply enough water and the vegetation was drying up. Abram assessed this situation and said that it was time to move down to Egypt. They would just make it on time, before the animals would give birth. The road was a relatively easy one, and it would just take a few weeks. Egypt! Sarai had heard about the gift of the Nile from the time she was a child. She had dreamed then about the stories recounting the flax fields, strange birds, sharp toothed huge reptiles in the river along with sea creatures bigger than horses spouting water through their nostrils.

As the caravan slowly moved along the Great Sea coast, they were stopped by Egyptian guards living in the shade of two stone pylons marked with hieroglyphics. The guards were merely checking to make sure that no enemy armies were sneaking into their country. Sheep herders were not of interest. But then as Sarai passed, striding with her head high as was her style, the men stared open-mouthed. How uncouth, she thought; at least in Ur the men looked at you in a more subtle manner. Maybe it was her clothing or hairstyle that made them stare. She didn't really pay attention as a rider galloped past them full speed in the direction of Memphis. But Abram had noticed the whole thing and fell into step along her, with a disturbed look on his face.

"Sarai, I have a bad feeling about this. You have no idea how beautiful you are. That's one of the attractive things about you. You think your nose is too big, your skin is too dark, your eyes are too wide apart. I know that you are stunning and now that we have descended into an idolatrous, sensuous country, the fact that you are beautiful will put me in danger."

"What are you saying, my husband?"

"This is a land where murder is not considered an evil. Say, therefore, upon being asked, that I am your brother. Say not that I am your husband for they will kill me and then take you to their king, the pharaoh. This way they will negotiate over brideswealth and perhaps by then my God will tell me what to do."

"But Abram, you have been teaching me the moral values of truth, and the religious belief of total trust in God!"

"Then perhaps I'm not on the level of trust as I thought I was, I fear too much for you."

"But if they take me to the Pharaoh, what am I to do? How could I prevent him from possessing me?"

"Have faith, Sarai."

But her faith was shaken by being told to lie. Well, it wasn't really a total lie, for she was Abram's niece-cousin, and in Ur such a relationship was called a sisterly one. And in Haran, when she became matriarch of her own household, she gained the title "wife-sister". So she would just omit the wife part. That was a sin of omission rather than commission.

The caravan drew closer to the big city, camping on the outskirts, when a group of uniformed men rode up to the tents, led by a man who Sarai recognized from the desert outpost. There, he was pointing at her.

The men approached Abram and talked to him, but Sarai was frozen in place, knowing that Abram's fears were real.

She came forward as Abram signaled to her. "What is it, my brother?" she asked.

"These men would like to bring you to the Pharaoh. It is a great honor, my sister, to be chosen like this."

"But must I go immediately? It is not done that way where we come from."

"It seems that Egypt has different customs, especially in connection with the Pharaoh, who is considered a man-god."

Before she knew it, Sarai was taken by the men and put into an enclosed sedan chair carried by two Nubian slaves. She was in such shock that she barely noticed the marble and stone palace what she was led into, nor the huge statues of strange creatures lining the enormous hallways. Swiftly she was led through a series of doors, until she finally focused on where they had stopped: it was the most luxurious bathhouse she had ever seen. Her nostalgia for the safety of Ur became almost overwhelming, and she didn't move as the young giggling female slaves began to undress her. Fighting back her fears, she disengaged herself from them and, naked, entered the first pool. It was of perfect temperature and so large that she returned to her youthful playfulness without thinking and dived beneath the water. When she surfaced, all the women were gathered at the edge of the pool, some with worried looks. Sarai realized that most Egyptian women couldn't swim, just like most women of Ur. So she smiled at them, and dived under again. This time when she surfaced they all clapped. She relaxed, paddled to the slave women with the familiar small clay pots in front of them and allowed herself to be shampooed, massaged, and oiled. The slaves made admonishing sounds at her calloused feet and at her suntanned arms and neck, indicating by signs that Egyptians preferred white, soft-skinned women. Then other slaves took over and dressed her in an embarrassingly sheer linen robe lined with gold and purple embroidery. They even brought out some exquisite collar-like necklaces for her to choose from, but she rejected the jewelry. Her hair hung long and straight, and the women had clipped the front into bangs, Egyptian style. Another woman applied kohl to her eyes and some kind of vermillion paste to her lips. When the two Nubian girls brought forward a large copper mirror and held it up, Sarai did not recognize herself. A door opened at the side, and suddenly all the women were flat on their faces, silent. A thin man—totally bald and hairless, of medium height, in a short white linen skirt and a large jeweled collar, holding a gold handled fly whisk—entered the room and slowly approached her. She stiffened, staring straight ahead. He walked around her twice, nodded approvingly, and left. As soon as the door closed after him the women got up, chattering to her, but she understood nothing until she made out one word: Pharaoh.

"That was Pharaoh?" she asked, and they all nodded. "Oh no," Sarai thought, "what do I do now?"

Nothing more happened that day. Sarai did not know that Pharaoh was arranging the payment of a kingly brideswealth for her: sheep, goats, donkeys, asses, camels as well as slaves. Abram, passing himself off as Sarai's brother and therefore empowered to arrange her marriage, could not turn down this offer, or he would risk his life. While he worried about Sarai, his faith in God's protection suddenly strengthened and overwhelmed him.

In the palace, Sarai understood that she was to be brought to the Pharaoh that night. She fearfully waited in the women's quarters. As she watched the goings-on in a distracted way, she noticed some strange things happening. The women all seemed to be getting their period, accompanied by terrible cramps. The few pregnant wives and concubines started having early labor pains, with the Pharaoh's youngest concubine on the verge of hysteria. In the midst of all the wailing and whimpering, two eunuchs came to fetch Sarai, but they were disconcerted by all the upheaval. Upon bringing her to the Pharaoh's room right next to the main women's, the Pharaoh heard the wailing too, and Sarai understood that he asked his eunuchs for an explanation. Upon hearing it, Pharaoh rose from his couch and walked slowly over to Sarai and speaking passable Semitic, asked her if she had anything to do with these bad things going on in his harem. "Are you a witch? Do you bring bad luck?" he asked. Before she could deny anything, Pharaoh himself turned a greenish color and rushed from the main room. Sarai could hear him throwing up in the vestibule. He re-entered the room and stalked over to Sarai, eyes flaming. "I know what is causing this! You are not that man's sister; you are his wife! This is all the punishment of the gods for adultery!" He ordered his eunuchs to fetch Abram.

Sitting on his throne, Pharaoh confronted Abram without any diplomatic niceties. "What is this you have done to me? Why did you not say that she," pointing to Sarai, "was your wife? Why did you say she was your sister, and so I took her for my wife? Here she is. Take her and go!"

Abram and Sarai bowed to Pharaoh, and Abram said that he was a prophet and would pray for him and his household. As they left the palace Sarai said, "Can he not kill you and then marry me, as you said?" "Not now," replied an ecstatic Abram, "for now it would shame him. He probably will even refuse the return of the brideswealth, as an act of generosity. Never mind that had he discovered our true relationship earlier, he would have had me killed." Glancing at his wife's outfit, as they were about to leave the palace, he quickly removed his outer cloak and wrapped her in it.

"Come, let us go to the encampment and properly thank God. I will pray for Pharaoh tonight. Tell me about your experience in the palace. It must have been dreadful." "Well, first I had a wonderful bath…" Sarai teasingly began.

* * *

As soon as word came from Canaan that the famine had ended, Abram, Sarai, and Lot returned from Egypt. The flocks were so large that uncle and nephew, to the joy of Sarai, decided to part company. God appeared to Abram to confirm this separation promising that Abram's descendants, not his nephew, would inherit the land. But ten years passed and Sarai still did not conceive. Abram's faith grew stronger and stronger, he made a Covenant with God, and had many inspiring prophecies. Sarai's faith was more realistic and down-to-earth. If Abram's descendants were to inherit the land, perhaps it would not be through her. She looked at her slave women with an assessing eye, evaluating their potential, and decided, albeit a bit hesitantly, on the Egyptian slave woman who had been sent to her by Pharaoh as a personal peace offering. Sarai had guessed from the start the Hagar was probably one of his many daughters born to a concubine, for the resemblance to her father was quite marked. But no one really said anything on the topic.

After some hard thinking, Sarai decided on her approach to Abram. She knew that if the topic were approached in the usual manner of equal partners discussing a problem, Abram would never agree to her plan. So she pulled matriarchal rank: in the Middle East the matriarch had complete control over issues that concerned women. "Abram," she began in a no-nonsense tone of voice, after they had finished supper and were resting in their shared tent. "God has prevented me from having a child. Take my slave Hagar as your secondary wife, and perhaps I will be built up through her." Her thought out words were perfect. She blamed only herself for not being able to conceive, and played on the acceptable idea of a matriarch, by adopting her slave's child, would build up her own family. By using a clever play on words, Sarai also implied that perhaps through this adoption she herself would be able to conceive, as anyone knowledgeable in these ways knew could happen.

Abram, recognizing both the tone and the logic, as well as the legal rights of the matriarch in this realm, reluctantly consented. So Sarai decisively took Hagar—before Sarai herself would change her mind—had the other slave women prepare her for her wedding night, and with a firmness that she really did not feel, presented Hagar to Abram herself. In withdrawing from the separate tent and returning to her own, Sarai was heavy hearted, but her desperation for a child overwhelmed her desire to Abram's one and only wife.

Less than a month later, the word began to go through the extended family that it was possible that Hagar had conceived. Within a few months it was definite. Abram's joy was boundless, and Sarai should have felt the same, but somehow her sacrifice was not working out quite as she had planned. Hagar began acting improperly and forgot from time to time that Sarai was her owner. Yes, some leeway could be given to early pregnancy crankiness and nausea, but it was the attitude that slowly became unbearable. It was as though she was saying, see what I could do and after all those years you could not. Why, she even looked like Pharaoh, with those Egyptian eyes evaluating her. No one could step out of line of proper behavior, or the whole power structure of the women's world would fall apart. Although she knew that she could alone make the decision to bring Hagar back in line, Sarai felt that since the unborn child was Abram's, he should agree to the chastisement.

"The wrong done to me be upon you," said Sarai to her husband, "I gave my slave to you and when she saw she had conceived, she denigrated me. May God judge between you and me."

Abram regarded his wife, and understanding why she had brought a women's issue to him, responded: "Here is your slave, she is in your power to do with her as you wish." And Sarai publicly castigated Hagar, causing her to run away from the campsite in shame and embarrassment. After a few hours passed and the temperature rose, Abram found Sarai supervising the slaves as they pounded the wheat into flour.

"Is she back?" he asked softly. "Not yet. She is working out how to swallow her pride." About an hour later, a small figure appeared in the distance slowly walking to the campsite. Hagar appeared, all sweaty and tired, with a chagrined yet excited look on her face. "My lord, my lady, I met a strange being who told me to return to you, to my proper place, and that I would bear a boy-child whose name would be Ishmael and who would grow into a wild proud man who would be in constant rivalry with all around him." Hagar went on and on, while Sarai thought to herself, "Fine. But I will not adopt your child. He will remain the son of a secondary wife."

By the end of the season, there was much rejoicing as Hagar gave birth to a son and Abram named him Ishmael. Only Sarai, while happy for her beloved husband, did not participate in her heart, although she did supervise preparing the feast, and she had supervised the birthing of the baby.

Thirteen years passed. Thirteen years of wandering with the flocks through Canaan. Thirteen years of honing the belief in God. Thirteen more years of barrenness for Sarai. She finally accepted her fate. At least she had her beloved husband to herself, although he did spend much time with Ishmael, instructing and discussing. But Sarai knew that although Ishmael put on a show of piety, he really was more influenced by his mother's Egyptian ways, and she had already caught him fooling around with some of the younger slave women. She had warned him away, and had warned Hagar, but Ishmael was the spoiled only son who thought he could do anything.

That night Abram woke Sarai in great excitement. He had just had one of his clearest prophetic experiences, and God had changed both their names—his to Abraham, hers to Sara. And they had made a covenant, to be marked by circumcision of all males, and best of all, the Lord had said that they—Abraham and Sara—were to have a child! Together! He told Sara that he had laughed with joy. What he didn't tell her was his sudden fear for Ishmael, and that the Lord had reassured him that Ishmael's descendants would form a great nation. Sara wanted to believe, and tried her best, but she was past menopause and who ever heard of a mature woman giving birth?

Meanwhile the entire household was agog as all of the males prepared for group circumcision, performed by Abraham with his sharpest flintstone. Sara and the skillful women provided balm and oils to help the healing, and hot wine with special medicinal herbs to ease the pain.

Such heat. Just three days after the group circumcision and all the boys and men lay in the shade of the tents, with the flaps half up to catch whatever breeze there was. "Abraham. Come in away from the tent opening and rest. You're not going to find anyone walking about in this heat."

"You are wrong, Sara. I see three men headed in our direction." He carefully stood up, limping a bit, but then regained his usual quick walking style as he rushed forward to greet the strangers and invite them to rest and refresh themselves. Abraham loved these unexpected visits and always expanded his knowledge of the surrounding lands and peoples and customs through the conversation with such strangers.

As usual, with their division of labor, Sara immediately moved to organize the women to bake the special cakes of hospitality. The flour had been pounded in the early morning, so it was simply a matter of adding water and some honey; the baking would be quick because the fire was already hot. Meanwhile Abraham rushed to the flock to choose a very young calf to be slaughtered and roasted while on the spit. While all of the food preparations proceeded, Abraham re-entered the tent to fetch the goat's milk and salty cheese made that morning that Sara had ready on the metal tray; these he himself served to the three men as they sat in the shade of the palm tree in front of the main tent. In good Middle Eastern custom, Sara did not serve strange men; this public arena was for men only.

The men drank the milk, ate some cheese, and within an hour the meat and cakes were served. Conversation was polite and the meal was generally eaten in silence. After washing off their fingers, the man in the middle politely asked, "Where is Sara, your wife?" What was going on? Thought Sara at the tent opening. They couldn't know her name, and it was totally unacceptable for any man to refer that way to a matriarch.

"In the tent," replied Abraham, also wondering about the strange turn of events. The stranger continued: "Next year at this time Sara your wife will have a boy-child."

Sara laughed to herself, knowing the biological ages of both herself and her husband. Then Sara experienced the Lord's presence, and a voice said, "Why do you laugh? Is anything too hard for Me?" Sara, in fear, began to deny her unbelieving laugh, but the voice again said, "You laughed in disbelief." Just then the three men arose to continue on their way, for they were the Lord's messengers sent to destroy the evil cities of Sodom and Gomorrah.

Sara remained in the tent as Abraham walked off with the three men, confused about her feelings. This was her first direct contact with the Lord—all her other experiences had been second-hand—and after much contemplation, realized that all the events of the past week were leading in the same direction. Abraham had a new dimension to himself with his new name and his circumcision; it was as though he had been reborn. Sara too had a new dimension with her new name, and her faith had just been cemented by direct contact with God. Perhaps, therefore, when Abraham returned to full strength, they would have a romantic night just like they used to. Now where were those perfumes?

The next morning the camp broke and they headed south to visit the Philistine city-state of Gerar. It would make a nice change from the Canaanite city-states, for word had it that the Philistines had originally come from across the Large Sea and had strange customs. Sara, feeling totally rejuvenated, strode alongside Abraham as they neared Gerar.

"I have a bad feeling," Abraham confessed. "I keep picturing our Egyptian experience of all those years ago."

"Nonsense. I was a young woman then. You and your bad feelings…"

"Sara, I have a premonition. Humor me. You have no idea how wonderful you look since the visit of God's messengers. Please, this is an immoral place where—like Egypt—murder is a lesser crime than adultery."

"So, I should say I'm your sister—just in case?"

Just then they entered the main gates of Gerar. The stone walls were high, and the fish-like gods stared down at them as the guard asked what their business was. The captain of the guard boldly eyed Sara as Abraham answered the questions.

"And who is this woman?" the captain asked.

"My sister," quickly responded Abraham, as they moved off into the city. After touring the bustling marketplace, Abraham and Sara walked to the center of the city to look at the main temple dedicated to the god Dagon.

"Interesting decorations and colors but not as sophisticated as Ur or Memphis," Sara began, when they heard a voice say, "There they are!" The nightmare again. Sara was taken by the captain of the guard and his men, leaving Abraham running after them until the palace gates were closed in his face.

Sara was brought directly into the throne room. A young man, black beard and hair trimmed very short, with a purple robe one, awaited her. Rising off the throne, Sara saw that he was extremely tall and quite thin.

"So, this is the new beauty you spotted for me? I do like mature women. Conversation with girls is boring. I'm so bored. Do you know any good stories? You look intelligent. Speak up—say something about yourself."

"My lord Avimelekh. I was born in Ur and have traveled from there to Haran, throughout Canaan, and down to Egypt."

"Wonderful. You'll tell me all about it tonight at dinner." Turning to the men, he said, "Give her to the women to prepare her."

Sara's nightmare had returned full force but not on as luxurious a level as in Egypt. She was bathed and perfumed, her hair was arranged, and she was dressed in a costly colorful robe. But now she knew, she just knew, that the Lord would save her. She waited to be called expecting a repeat of the Egyptian affair, for the women of the household had all begun to menstruate and miscarry, but morning came and she had not been sent for.

It was mid-morning before she was summoned, but not to the king's bedroom. She was brought into the throne-room where a very distraught Avimelekh was almost shouting at her husband in front of a gathering of important men and magicians and priests of Gerar.

"And then I had this terrible dream where your God warned me not to touch this woman or I would die for she was married. I answered your God—in the dream—that I was innocent because I had been told by him that she was his sister and by her that he was her brother. Your God then said that He knew I was innocent and therefore had prevented me from touching her. Finally your God said that I should return your wife to you and that you were a prophet who could cure me and all my women; if I did not I would die. What did I ever do to you that you should bring all this horror on me and my family?"

Abraham could not answer the truth, namely that the king had broken all rules of protocol by simply taking Sara and by not negotiating a marriage. Instead he said: "I said what I did for fear of this city where murder is a lesser crime than adultery. I feared I would be killed and my wife taken. And she is my sister in a way, for she is my niece and Semites raise the status of nieces to "sisters." She is my relative and my wife. My sin is that of omitting that she is also my wife."

Avimelekh turned to his ministers and ordered them to give Abraham sheep and cattle and slaves, and, turning to Sara, he motioned her to join her husband. As a final magnanimous gesture to Abraham the nomad, he said, "My land is before you; you are welcome to settle where you will."

To Sara he said as he reached into a carved box, "Here is a face decoration of a thousand pieces of silver. Wear it as proof that I never wronged you." Sara accepted the exquisite gift bowing slightly, looking him right in the eye. She hooked it on, and it formed a kind of tight-fitting bonnet, with some of the silver dangling on chains almost into her eyes. "Stunning," Avimelekh signed softly. Abraham prayed to God to heal the king and all his wives. As they left the palace the constant wailing and keening from the women's quarters stopped.

"What now my wife?" asked Abraham.

"Well, I'm all bathed, perfumed, dressed, and decorated. Let's go back to our humble tent."

A few weeks later Sara told Abraham that they should stay at their campsite a few more days as she was not feeling well. The next morning she still felt awful. And the next. Her slaves brought her hot drinks, cool damp cloths, and sympathy, until her oldest slave looked at her and started laughing.

"What is so funny? I feel horrible," complained Sara.

"My lady, you only feel awful in the morning hours. Then you eat like there is no tomorrow. And you crave salty almonds and pomegranate juice. You are pregnant!"

"Impossible," said Sara, but not so impossible if you believe in the power of God. Sara spent the next nine months in a cocoon of joy, sensating every new feeling, humming as the child-to-be kicked or punched or turned over. So this is what it was like. Abraham hovered over her ready to bring her anything to help her walk or sit or get up. Getting up was the hardest part.

Then came the muscle spasms. She went into her tent, surrounded by all her women. The birth was easy, just a few major pushes and the baby was out. Everyone was yelling with excitement. "A boy, a man-child, an heir!"

Abraham rushed in to hold his newborn, joy lighting his entire face. "Isaac. Isaac because I laughed, you laughed and we all laugh with happiness." He returned the baby to his drowsy wife and chuckled as the infant already began making sucking noises.

Eight days later Abraham circumcised his son, making a huge feast. The women gathered almost unbelievingly in the women's quarters watching as Sara nursed her son. "So it is true. He's not adopted. No woman who has not birthed can nurse."

Everything was ready. Sara checked all the food one more time. Fruit, nuts, seeds, roast meat, breads, cakes, juices, cool water, wine. The trays were heaped high and the guests were beginning to arrive.

In typical Middle Eastern style, Abraham and Sara were celebrating the weaning of Isaac, who was now a strapping four-year-old. The cause for the celebration was simple: everyone knew that the first four years of a child's life were the crucial ones. If he survived all the childhood illnesses and dangers, the probability was that he would reach adulthood. Also, weaning meant he was leaving the women's quarters for the male world. He would now learn how to hunt, how to ride horses, animal husbandry, and trading. He had been brought up believing in God so that the personal journeys of his parents would not be repeated.

Sara looked into the men's area, to make sure that the slaves were serving properly. She was about to turn her attention to her women guests when a movement caught her eye. She stepped under the tent ropes and over the stakes, to find Ishmael in a lusty embrace with one of the slave women, whose robe was half off her body. A few feet away she saw her son standing open-mouthed, watching.

"Away," she ordered Isaac. "Your father awaits you," as the child scampered off. "As for you," she said to the unembarrassed seventeen-year-old with the Egyptian uptilted eyes, "you will suffer for this."

"What will you do, oh great one, eject the first-born son of Abraham?" he sneered.

"Exactly," she replied turning her heel, but not before seeing the look of fear on his face.

Sara waited until the celebration was over. Choosing the right moment, she approached her husband. "I want you to banish my slave woman and her son, for I do not want the son of this slave to inherit with my son Isaac."

Abraham noted the careful choice of words. Sara was implying, by not even naming Ishmael, but by referring to him as "the son of the slave" that Hagar's influence was stronger than his. He also knew that the inheritance that Sara was referring to was not the wealth—there was enough for ten sons—but the spiritual inheritance, the God-believing lineage. He was very upset because in his heart he knew that Sara was right. That night the Lord confirmed to Abraham that Sara was right but that he shouldn't fear for Ishmael, for he would be the progenitor of a great nation.

The next morning Abraham took bread and a leather flask of water, enough to last several days, and gave them to Hagar. Ishmael was a hunter and a fighter who could protect his mother as they walked towards Beersheba, the nearest big oasis. He gave then silver and a small parchment declaring that Hagar was a free woman, so that no one would presume that she was a runaway slave. Ishmael tried one more time to beg his father to change his mind, but with tears in his eyes, Abraham embraced his son one last time.

Sara stayed in the tent comforting Isaac over the loss of his big half-brother, whom he adored and followed everywhere. "But why, why must they leave?"

"You'll understand some day. I hope you will never have to make such a decision," murmured Sara, relieved beyond words that at last Ishmael's bad influence would be removed forever. She could now relax. She hummed to herself as she reread the parchment sent from Haran relating the family news, that Abraham's brother had eight sons over the years, and that one son, Betuel, had one son and one daughter. "A cousin for Isaac to marry, perhaps. I hope I live to see it," she thought.

But she did not. A few years later, upon hearing Abraham recount how he almost offered Isaac up to God as a final test in his belief, Sara's heart stopped beating, and instead of shared joy, Abraham descended into the depths of sorrow as he set about finding a burial place for his beloved partner. He bought the sepulcher at Kiryat Arba, better known as Hebron, signing a contract for it with Ephron in front of all the town leaders. He told Isaac that when he died, he too wished to be buried next to his only wife. Isaac, numb from shock at the loss of his mother, and still in a state of spiritual upheaval at the experience of almost dying himself, simply nodded. The two walked off towards the campsite as one.

Notes

The Biblical texts for this chapter are Genesis 11:26-32, and Genesis 12–22:1-2.

For background material I recommend William H. Stiebling, *Ancient Near Eastern History and Culture* (Routledge, 2016); Michal Dayagi-Mendels, *Perfumes and Cosmetics in the Ancient World* (The Israel Museum, 1989); Philip J. King and Lawrence Stager, *Life in Biblical Israel* (John Knox Press, 2001); and Carol L. Meyers, *Discovering Eve: Ancient Israelite Women in Context* (Oxford University Press, 1988). The most detailed book is Jennie R. Ebeling, *Women's Lives in Biblical Times* (T & T Clark International, 2010), especially chapters 4, 5, and 6.

Rebecca

The household was just beginning to stir. The sun wasn't up yet, but Rebecca felt her mother move on the pallet next to hers, and the cool morning air that touched her as the covering moved caused her to cuddle further down for warmth. She tried to hold on to her dream but it slipped away. She only remembered its familiarity, as though she had already dreamed it, vaguely picturing camels and traveling.

"I wish," she thought as she awoke completely: "What I would give to travel away from Haran and the walls with ears." She glanced around the small room that she shared with her mother. It was luxurious enough, by Haran standards, decorated with woven carpets and wall hangings, with all her robes neatly piled on one side, and her mother's on the other side of the narrow table. Her mother had a small inlaid box with her jewels in it, hidden deep in the pile of folded robes. Rebecca sometimes pulled it out, and admired each item. She also checked out her mother's face creams, kohl, and tiny bottles of perfume.

"Some day," she sighed. "But I will not agree to marry one of the local boys…. As if father would listen….well, not father as much as that brother of mine. I hate him. All he thinks about is how rich he will be when a marriage will be arranged for me. Watch them marry me off to some old ugly man with ten other wives! I'll run away… I'll…"

"Rebecca! Up, up. Time to prepare the first meal. You are doing the entire first meal yourself today. Come, it's easy."

Her mother handed her a robe of undyed wool, but decorated with some red embroidery. After all, it would not look good to have Bethuel's daughter dressed like a slave. Her mother quickly twisted the loose braids into a knot, and gently pushed Rebecca out of the door into the main family compound. They crossed the central open section to the cooking area where the slaves had already started the fire.

Rebecca gave the orders to the slaves as to how to prepare the flat breads, and supervised the mixing of the ingredients as well as the size of the balls of dough taken to be flattened out, put on the board and gently pushed into the oven. She checked the baking, telling the oldest slave when to pull out the finished bread. Meanwhile, she dipped a ladle into the cool crockery pot where the yoghurt was kept, and ordered a slave to cut up the cucumbers. The youngest slave came back from the chicken coop holding six eggs in a kerchief. These were placed in a pot already half filled with water and hung on a hook over the fire near the oven. The large low tray in a corner of the public area was filled with the fresh food just as the men came out of their rooms ready to eat. They ate without any conversation, arose from the carpets and walked out of the front gate of the compound heading for the fields, where Laban would go to look after the flocks, and Bethuel would check on the planted areas. Rebecca, her mother and the household slaves had their meal, her mother complimenting Rebecca on a job well done.

"You are ready to run your own household. I've done my job. You also are old enough. Let us see who the gods will bring. Meanwhile today is a spinning, weaving and embroidering day for you. The slaves will do the washing and cleaning. And, Rebecca, remember before you disappear, this evening it's your turn to fetch the water at the central well. Remember to stand very straight or the jug will fall, like last time."

The day passed, as all Rebecca's days passed, filled with work and dreams. As the sun moved towards the west, she went to the cooking area to fetch the large empty clay jar, which at one time was larger than she, but now that she had grown, reached only up to her waist. She gracefully lifted it to her shoulder making sure that she had the matted piece of cloth tied around her waist, which would later serve as a kind of shock absorber as she carried the full jug on her head.

"I wonder what's new in town," she thought as she left the compound. "I'll soon know because all the unmarried girls will be there this evening. At least we get out once a day. I think my father would lock me away if not for the town's pressure. He claims that in Ur—which he never saw—young women never went out unsupervised. As if going to the well was unsupervised! How much more public can you be."

Rebecca descended the winding pathway to the open market where the well was located, just inside the walls of Haran. "It looks a bit crowded today. Perhaps a caravan has arrived! Maybe from Egypt or from the two rivers or even from nearby Canaan."

She quickened her pace, for she saw that the other young women were already descending into the deep well single file; some were already emerging slowly from the other side of the well, their full jars carefully balanced on their heads.

"Well, that looks like a stranger, all dusty, near the entrance to the well. He seems to be looking at all the women... just like in my dream," Rebecca remembered with a start. "He certainly is looking at me in a very strange way. He looks Canaanite, to judge by his clothing, and rich."

She descended into the half light of the well. The damp smell was as always, and she knelt to lower her jug into the gurgling cold water. She then lifted the jug, first to her shoulder level, then, having placed the thick cloth on her head, she lifted the heavy weight onto it. Standing carefully, with her right hand balancing the load, she felt the stairs leading up rather than saw them. Up into the evening air, and there was the strange man awaiting her.

"Please, may I have some water to drink from your jug," said the stranger in a polite manner.

"Certainly, please drink my lord," Rebecca replied, hurrying to lower the heavy jar, and pouring him some into his small clay cup. As he drank, she examined him, noticing the heavy dust on his clothing and his feet. Glancing behind him, she realized that the ten or so camels kneeling nearby were also covered with dust and their nostrils were pricked up in the direction of the scent of the water.

"Are those your camels, my lord?"

"Yes, we have just arrived from Canaan."

"Then they must be thirsty too. In our land we give our animals drink and food before ourselves. Please allow me to give them to drink as well." And without waiting for a response, Rebecca emptied the jug into the trough that was perpendicular to the well. The camels came slowly to the trough after noisily rising, at the signal of the man to the slaves sitting with the camels. Rebecca rushed up and down the narrow stairs of the well with jugs of water until the trough was full and the camels had drunk their fill. Tired, she descended on last time to fetch the water that she was responsible for. On reaching the surface, the stranger awaited her.

"I must return home or they will wonder what kept me."

"Please, you have been so kind and generous," he said, "I have something for you." Before Rebecca could move away the man took out a delicate gold nose ring and two intricately worked heavy gold bracelets.

"Whose daughter are you, please, and is there room in your father's house for us to spend the night?"

Rebecca eyed the golden jewelry, and, looking the man straight in the eye, using her own judgment, replied: "I am the daughter of Bethuel, son of Milca, wife of Abraham's brother Nahor; we have plenty of straw and feed for your animals as well as place to sleep."

The stranger bowed before her, as she rushed away after putting on the gold gifts, and through the corner of her eye she noticed him bowing all the way to the earth as she rushed uphill in her excitement to share the news and inform her father. Bursting into her mother's quarters and lowering the water jug, she forestalled the angry questions by quickly summarizing what had happened to her startled mother and father.

Laban rushed out ahead of Bethuel to greet the stranger at the well. Rebecca knew that his alacrity was not based on generosity but on greed, for she had noticed how he examined her golden gifts. Laban returned shortly with the stranger, the slaves following behind with the camels, which were put into the compound and fed.

Meanwhile the women of the household rushed to prepare for the unexpected extra five men. A lamb was slaughtered and quickly prepared for roasting on the open spit, while extra amounts of rice were put into the large pot to boil, and vegetables washed and cut up. By the time the camels had been attended to, the meal was ready, and the stranger was led to the guest area while his slaves went into the male slaves' quarters.

Rebecca, her mother and the women slaves were agog with excitement, but the male slaves served the food to the stranger while the women tried to overhear the conversation.

"I beg your indulgence," the stranger said to Bethuel, "for breaking protocol, but I would prefer to speak before I eat." Rebecca felt a shiver go through her spine as the stranger started his story upon the nod from her father. "I am Abraham's slave."

"Abraham," she thought, "my grandfather's brother! The one who did those strange things, and worships one God! This has to do with me—I know it in my bones."

"God has blessed my lord with riches and late in life he and his wife Sara had a son, an heir. My master made me—for I am in charge of the household—swear that I would never take a Canaanite wife for Isaac, but that I would travel to Haran to take a wife from his family there. I responded: 'What if the woman will not agree to come to Canaan, for it is her right to refuse to move away from her birthplace.' My lord responded that his God would assure my success. I arrived today at the well and prayed to my master's God to help me, for the quality in a wife that I desired was kindness. Therefore the sign of my success would be if the young woman from whom I asked a drink would volunteer to water my camels as well."

The stranger paused, and Rebecca felt a surge of happiness flow through her, for she anticipated the rest of the speech.

"Before I completed my request of my lord's God, Rebecca came to the well with her jug on her shoulder. I watched her descend into the well, looking so aristocratic, that when she climbed up on the other side, I put to her my request for a drink. She not only rushed to lower her heavy water jug, saying "please drink," but rushed also to water the camels. Then I asked her whose daughter she was, and when she told me that she was Nahor's granddaughter, I knew that I had found a perfect bride. I gave her the nose ring and gold bracelets as a preliminary gift, bowing to my lord's God. I want the betrothal agreed to right now, for if you do not agree, I do not want to waste time but will search elsewhere."

Laban and Bethuel spoke together, reassuring the stranger. "This is from God." "How can we speak ill or good about such a thing: here is Rebecca—take her and go, and let her be your master's son's wife as God said."

Rebecca was ecstatic! She would finally get out of this house and away from her awful brother. What brideswealth was he pulling out of the camelpacks! Silver bowls, and gold bowls, and presents for Laban and her mother, and gorgeous clothing of fine wool and others of fine linen for her.

The men sat down to eat and celebrate the conclusion of the betrothal negotiations, drinking much wine along with the festive meal. The stranger then went off to sleep in the guest area, tired from his long trip, but the household itself stirred with excitement well into the night. Rebecca dreamed her dream again, but this time, as she awoke early, she realized it was no longer a dream. She rushed to help prepare breakfast, and almost bumped into Abraham's slave as she set up the food in the man's area. When her father and brother came in, he said to them: "I am breaking protocol again, for I would like permission to take Rebecca to Canaan today."

"Today," her brother and mother said in unison. "We need at least a week to prepare her for her trip and to say farewell."

"Please do not delay me but allow me to return immediately to my master."

"This is really against our custom, but why not just ask Rebecca since she has to agree to move so far away and so soon."

Rebecca was sent for, and, standing in front of the stranger, her father and her brother, answered yes, that she agreed to leave at once for Canaan.

For the next four hours or so the house was in utter upheaval as her mother ran from room to room, ordering the slaves to pack this and that as Rebecca's household goods and presents, and her father and brother argued over which slaves to give her as a wedding present. Laban won out and only four young slave women were sent, along with Rebecca's old nanny who had been her wetnurse when she was an infant. This way she would have at least one confidant in the strange household, and would not miss home too much.

As the camels were loaded, and Rebecca atop a camel, rose up into the air high above her family, she heard them blessing her with the traditional blessings of fertility and power. She waved to her parents and friends, and with excited anticipation left the gates and walls of Haran behind on her way to a new life.

Five days later, sore from the camel saddle, but content with viewing the scenery, Rebecca asked Abraham's slave if the trip would last much longer.

"No," he responded with an understanding smile. "See, the trees have thinned out and the desert of the Negev is beginning. We may actually make it to the camp by sundown."

"Oh, I can't wait to have a real bath," sighed Rebecca, examining the sparse vegetation and the open vistas in front of her. The sun continued on its path through the sky, and as it reached the western edge, where Abraham's slave, Eliezer, had said there was a boundless sea, Rebecca saw the shape of a man in the distance. Squinting into the setting sun, it seemed to her that the man was rapidly walking towards the caravan. "How unusual," she thought. "No one goes out alone here. Let me ask Eliezer." She dropped off the side of her camel and hurried to Eliezer who was walking at the head of the caravan. "Who is that man walking in the fields toward us? Do you know him?"

Squinting into the setting sun, Eliezer responded, "It is my young master! He must have seen the caravan and is coming to greet us to see if I have been successful."

But Rebecca was no longer there; she had rushed back to her camel to remove the traditional betrothal veil from the pack. Wrapping herself in the gauzy material, she was now ready to meet her husband-to-be. With heart beating she waited for him to come closer so that she could see what he looked like, for she only had Eliezer's verbal description of his master. He had been entertaining her the entire trip with stories of her new family, and she was only sorry that she could never meet Isaac's mother.

Isaac greeting Eliezer warmly, but his eyes were searching for her. He spied the veil and smiled shyly in her direction, not greeting her directly, as protocol dictated.

The caravan reached the huge campsite just as the last rays of the sun disappeared. The big fire in the center was a welcoming sight, and as the camels knelt to be unloaded and unhitched, an old stately man walked over to greet Eliezer. "Here she is, my lord," said a bowing Eliezer, indicating Rebecca, quickly telling him of his wonderful good fortune in finding her. "Rebecca, dear child. Dear grandchild of my brother! Come, let me look at you. Isaac, go away so that she can remove her betrothal veil in front of me. That's it—wait near the eating area. Ah, my dear young woman, you are a sight for sore eyes. Come, let me embrace you."

Rebecca almost cried with joy at Abraham's greeting. Finally she would be appreciated and loved, not only by a husband but by a father-in-law.

"We will let you rest a few days and then the marriage will be completed. Is that agreeable with you?"

"Yes, father-in-law. I will be ready in two days" time."

"Excellent. Meanwhile this is your temporary tent, to use in your preparations. I have provided all the female things that I remembered that my wife used to use. It is all yours now. I even found some perfumes from Ur that I had bought for Sara years and years ago. I see that you have brought your own personal slaves with you. That is a good idea, but you will find that my slaves are most accommodating and agreeable. Sara trained them well. The women's world awaits its new matriarch."

"Matriarch! I'm a little young for that title and responsibility." Looking at her, Rebecca felt that Abraham's eyes penetrated to her soul. He smiled a knowing smile. "You will do fine, with the women's world and with my son. He's not an easy man, having been a bachelor for so long, but you are intelligent and will learn how to manage him. Now, wash up, eat, and try to sleep. The desert air is wonderfully refreshing."

For the next two days Rebecca was pampered and prepared for her marriage night, as the entire camp busied itself with the food preparations. As if in her dream, Rebecca allowed the slaves to fuss over her, as she chose which robe and which jewelry to wear. Finally, she was led from her tent, with her face covered by a web-thin betrothal veil, to take Isaac's hand in front of the invited crowd. Seeing his face light up with joy, she knew that he was pleased. He was a little older than she had anticipated, for he was forty, but that was all right, since she already knew that he was gentle and kind.

The crowd sang and the women ululated as Isaac led her to Sara's luxurious tent, which was now to be Rebecca's.

Twenty years passed. As Rebecca awoke early, listening to the rustle of the animals, she reviewed in her mind the events of the past two decades. Her beloved father-in-law's death, the arrival of Ishmael for the interment in the double sepulcher cave in Hebron, the tension until he left, the slow traveling through Canaan, and the gradually evolving and maturing faith in the one God. She slipped out from the warmth of the covers, dressed quickly, and stepped out of her tent into the brisk desert air. As she walked to the cooking area, to supervise the food preparation, she saw with surprise that her husband was walking down from the protecting hill to the east of the campsite. Greeting him while giving the slaves their instructions, she looked at him inquiringly. He had a self-satisfied look on his face, and hummed to himself as he helped himself to a freshly baked bread and some fragrant goat cheese. "You're in a good mood," Rebecca said. "Yes, I had a wonderful conversation with my Lord," was all Isaac would say. "Is there any hot mint tea? It's chilly this morning. Oh Rebecca, I hope to visit your tent tonight, if the time is right."

Blushing, and furious with herself for doing so, Rebecca nodded, grateful that he was giving her time to prepare. This time, instead of using love potions and Canaanite talismans, Rebecca had a conversation in her mind with Isaac's God. "Surely, it's time. I know that Abraham and Sara were childless for longer, but surely twenty years is long enough for us to learn that fertility depends on You, and that all three of us produce a child. Twenty years? I rely on You, the God of Abraham and Isaac."

Upon entering her tent that night, Isaac told her that that morning God had assured him that they would soon have a child. Isaac's faith was total, and Rebecca felt it influencing her as well. "Perhaps God was waiting for my faith to be complete as well," she thought as she brought her husband some hot wine with cloves and cinnamon in it. The spicy odor filled the tent and they both smiled happily at each other. "This time it will work, I know it," she thought.

A month later, Rebecca informed Isaac that she thought she was pregnant. A month after that she was sure. Isaac fussed over her, and wanted to slow down the pace of their travels, but she told him that she felt fine. If anything she had so much energy she didn't know what to do with it.

At five months, Rebecca started to feel very heavy. She looked at her expanding belly and said to herself, "This isn't normal. I'm enormous at only five months. And I'm in pain. Pains shouldn't come for another four months." Deborah, her slave woman who had been her wetnurse, put perfumed oils on Rebecca's belly, telling her that every pregnancy was different. So, for another month Rebecca carried on, pretending that all was well.

At seven months, however, she felt that her belly was being punched and kicked from inside. It was non-stop. The midwife checked her, Deborah tried to calm her, and Isaac stayed out of her way. It finally was just too much to bear, and Rebecca slowly climbed the low mountain that Isaac mounted whenever he felt the need to communicate with the Lord. At the peak, she found the altar that Isaac used for his divine offerings. Breathing heavily from the exertion of climbing, she waddled over to the altar, addressing God as if he were in front of her. "What is going on, oh Lord? Why am I in such pain? You said to Isaac that this time he would have a child!"

Leaning on the altar, she lowered herself onto a conveniently placed rock, and relaxed against the huge boulder next to it. The strong sun and exertion of the climb had the effect of putting her into a half-sleep. Softly she felt a voice such as she had never heard before. "You are pregnant with two distinct children, and two nations will emerge from you who will constantly be rivals, and the elder shall serve the younger." The voice ceased, and Rebecca realized with a start that the Lord had spoken to her directly for the first time. She arose slowly and carefully worked her way back down the mountain to the campsite, content that she finally had an explanation for her difficult pregnancy. Yet the more she thought about God's message the more she realized that it was more than just an explanation; it was a prophecy for the future that would direct her entire life.

At nine months exactly the midwife was sent for. The pains were different and growing in frequency. Deborah held Rebecca's hand as the midwife showed her how to sit on the birthstool. Leaning back on the stool with the midwife kneeling in front of her, she let her body push the first baby out. He was large, and when the midwife held him up, Rebecca got a quick look at a red hairy body before the pains turned her attention back to the twin, whose hand was grasping the first one's heel as he emerged from her body. "Unbelievable," she heard the midwife murmur, as the second son, smooth as could be, was held up for Rebecca to see.

Isaac came rushing into the tent as soon as he was informed that the births were completed. Looking from one son to the other, he name his first born Esau and his second born Jacob, the names becoming official eight days later at their circumcisions. Isaac kissed his tired wife affectionately, whispering private words of love and happiness. Rebecca drifted off into a well-deserved sleep, thinking as she floated away, "I hope I have enough milk for both…"

The boys grew and filled the campsite with their noise and competition over everything. Esau remained a hairy boy, growing into an avid hunter. Isaac admired the physical presence of his first-born as well as his hunting abilities. As he grew older, Isaac's vision faded more and more, and Esau's descriptions of his escapades was great entertainment. He chose not to see that Esau's belief in God was superficial, that he never discussed it with his father, and that he was geared almost totally to physical and quick gratifications. Jacob, while as large and strong as Esau—proven over and over in their childhood wrestlings—did not enjoy hunting, but preferred the life of the extensive tents, supervising the flocks and learning all that he could from everyone. He had long discussion about God with his father, and came to his own understanding at an early age. He was straightforward in his relationships, but masterful at the same time. Rebecca loved him with all her being, recognizing his goodness, intelligence and true kindness. She saw Esau for what he was, seeing her own brother in him and therefore preferring Jacob. She also remembered her prophecy, and could not understand Isaac's preference for his wild son, Esau. The topic had been discussed by the two of them over and over, with Isaac absolutely refusing to see that Esau was the wrong son for carrying on God's work. Rebecca had given up trying to convince him, confident that God's plan would prevail. Just then the issue of survival was more important as a famine had just developed in Canaan.

"Are we to go to Egypt?" the young men asked Isaac. "No. I have been ordered not to go out of Canaan. We will go instead to Gerar. Avimelech gave my father the right to settle there at any time; hopefully the promise will also apply to me."

The pack animals were loaded up, the flocks gathered into tight groups, and the entire camp headed south towards the Philistine city-state of Gerar.

"Rebecca."

"Yes, I am here."

"I can see you clearly in this bright sunshine and I see that you are as beautiful as when I first saw you. I have a bad feeling about the Philistines, for my father taught me that they are so immoral, that they consider murder a lesser crime than adultery."

"So? What does that have to do with me? Oh no, Isaac, are you going to ask me to do what your mother did? Look at what almost happened to her! Where is your faith?

"Please, Rebecca. King Avimelekh may be a much older man now, but he is just as lascivious."

As they approached the city walls of Gerar, they had to pass through a checkpoint. The soldiers looked at Rebecca and asked Isaac who she was.

"My sister," responded Isaac. They let the group pass into the city-state, and Isaac heaved a sigh of relief. "They aren't bothering us," he said softly to Rebecca.

"Wait," she responded.

A few days later, Rebecca said to Isaac that she felt that she was constantly being watched. Isaac said that it was her imagination. To prove his point, as they walked down a narrow street right next to the palace, he grabbed her in a loving hug, kissing her in a most unbrotherly way.

"Isaac, what has come over you? Someone might see us!"

From the heights of his private room in the palace Avimelekh saw this exchange. He had been watching the couple for the past week, lusting after Rebecca but with a clear memory of Isaac's mother and the unfortunate (for him) experiences connected with Sara. When his men had informed him of the arrival of a beautiful woman with her brother, he had decided to wait and watch. He immediately sent for Isaac and Rebecca to appear before him.

Terrified, Rebecca walked alongside her husband into the Philistine palace. She barely noticed the thick columns, the fish-like idols, and the armed guards. After what seemed like an endless corridor, she found herself in the throne room, where an old man dressed in a magnificent blue robe was seated. As she and Isaac were motioned to approach the throne, she saw his thick lips and looked into his angry black eyes.

He directed his comments to Isaac, but he kept his eyes on Rebecca. Without any introduction, he growled, "Why didn't you say that this woman was your wife? Why did you say she was your sister?"

"I was told that had I said she was my wife, I could have been killed and my wife taken away," responded Isaac clearly.

"What have you done?" the king almost shouted. "One of my people almost took you wife as his wife, and that would have brought shame on all of us!"

Rebecca realized that the king meant himself, as his black eyes raked her up and down. She turned bright red at the thought, but held her head high, as Isaac took a breath to respond.

"Tell everyone," the king continued, looking at his advisers and officers, "that no one is to touch this man nor this woman on pain of death." Avimelekh took it for granted that Isaac had inherited Abraham's powers of prophecy and feared them. "Now leave us, but your father's welcome is extended to you as well," he concluded, dismissing Rebecca and Isaac.

They left the court elated, and Isaac, now with official permission, settled for many years on the outskirts of the city-state. He succeeded in digging his own wells for his flocks, and with this assured water supply, the family settled down and the years passed.

Isaac began to feel old -- not that he was terribly old, but he felt that way and acted that way. Rebecca was convinced that it had to do with Esau's suddenly coming home with his two Hittite wives, shocking Isaac, but not enough to change his views towards his favorite son. It was Rebecca who had to bear the brunt of the two women in her realm as matriarch. They were not only uncooperative, but they laughed behind her back about the morality taught by the Lord. Rebecca also felt that Isaac's aging had to do with his ever rapidly decreasing vision. He was almost completely blind and hated relying on others for even the simplest thing.

She was in the back of Isaac's tent folding up various fabrics and household goods, when the flap of the tent flashed open and Esau strode in. Rebecca stood absolutely still, counting in Esau's sudden blindness upon entering the dark tent to hide her completely, so that she could overhear the conversation which could prove to be important. She knew that Isaac was worried about something, but he had not confided in her.

"You sent for me, father?"

"Is that you, Esau? I have been aging rapidly and do not know when I will die. Go out and hunt for a deer or mountain goat, cooking it into my favorite dish. After eating it I will bless you with the blessing of the first born."

Esau left immediately, and Rebecca hurried out as well.

"Quick, quick," she rushed into Jacob's tent. "I overheard your father telling Esau that he would give him the first born's blessing as soon as he had eaten from the food that he would make. We don't have much time." She forced Jacob to face her. "You must listen to me, for as your mother I demand your obedience in this instance. Go immediately to the flock and bring me two newborn kids. I will cook them with your father's favorite spices and you will bring the dish to him so that he will bless you before his death."

"Mother, you are overlooking Esau's and my physical differences. He is hairy and I am smooth. What will happen if Father chooses to touch me; then I will be a sinner and bring upon myself a curse and not a blessing."

Rebecca answered, "Upon me your curse," knowing full well that as a grown man Jacob was responsible for himself, but she felt she had to say something. "Just listen and obey me now! For once, no discussion."

Jacob realized there was no arguing with his mother. Besides, hadn't Esau traded him his birthright for lentil soup all those years ago? Such an exaggerator, his brother was, first by claiming he was dying of hunger and then by trading his birthright for food. That just showed you how little it meant to him, whereas to Jacob it meant everything to be blessed with the religious continuity of his father and grandfather.

Rebecca took the freshly killed and butchered young kids and as quickly as she could, gave instructions to the slaves to prepare the spicy dish. Meanwhile she went into her tent to take out Esau's best clothing in which to dress Jacob. She certainly wasn't going to have those two Hittite women responsible for the valuable robes. Looking at him, she frowned, and solved the hairlessness problem of the arms and neck of Jacob by placing the soft yet hairy skins of baby goats on these bare spots. The slaves motioned that the food was ready, so Rebecca gave the hot dish to Jacob, encouraging him with the whisper, "Remember what God said to me: "the elder shall serve the younger!" But God only helps those who help themselves, so be strong."

Rebecca waited outside with bated breath, looking out towards the wilderness to check if Esau was returning with his kill. "How much longer do we have? Please use those brains of yours, Jacob my love. You may have to lie, my moral upright son, but the blessing is worth it. And this may be the only way I can prove to your father how blind he has been to Esau all these years. Here he comes with his kill. Jacob, please hurry."

Jacob stepped out of the tent just then, and Rebecca hurried him immediately into her own tent right next door. She quickly stripped off Esau's robe and the skins, while Jacob summarized what had happened. He was ecstatic and terrified at the same time.

"Stay here until I see what's happening," she whispered as she rushed out and stepped into her husband's tent just in time to hear Esau say to Isaac, "I am your first born son, Esau." She saw Isaac shudder throughout his whole body as he realized what had happened, and that if he had been fooled so easily then perhaps Rebecca was right about Esau's character as well.

"Then who was it whose food I ate and whom I blessed, and who shall remain blessed?"

Knowledge dawned on Esau of what had happened and he began to cry loudly and bitterly. "Bless me too father, bless me too," he wailed just like a spoiled child, and for once because of his emotional state, his tongue slipped in front of his father and he added, "He is just like his name, my brother Jacob, for he manipulated me twice now, first by stealing my birthright and now my blessing. Please father, please bless me!"

Rebecca quietly left the tent, convinced that her husband had finally realized his errors, especially since Esau himself had referred to the trade for his birthright. Isaac had absolutely refused to listen to her about that trade all these years. But now she feared for Jacob's safety, for Esau, out of control, could very easily kill his twin. Now, how could she manipulate Jacob into going away? He loved her too much to go of his own will. Why did she always have to manipulate her men? Why couldn't she have open relationships like her long-dead mother-in-law, Sara? Just then her glance fell on Esau's despicable wives, as they whispered to each other, always plotting. She hated them, but at least she now had an idea.

Re-entering her tent she saw her beloved son, in whose face she saw her own features, but with Isaac's luminous eyes. "Good news and bad. The good news is that your father is well aware of what happened and you are to retain the blessing." Drawing a deep breath, she continued. "The bad news is that Esau means to kill you. Listen to me, my son. I know how hard this is, but you must flee to my brother's home in Haran. It will only be for a short time, until your brother's vicious temper cools and he forgets what you did." She grabbed Jacob's dark head to keep it from shaking no from side to side. "Go! I will send for you as soon as it is safe." Rebecca used her ultimate weapon to finally convince her reluctant son. "How could I survive if I lose both of you at once?" Guilt always worked.

Rebecca had one more hurdle, namely convincing Isaac that it was his idea to send Jacob to her brother's home. After all, patriarchal pride was at stake, and Rebecca was wise enough to let her manipulations of her husband be discrete. Walking into his tent, she ignored his distraught state by bemoaning her lot with the awful Hittite wives of Esau. "I can't stand them. If Jacob married one of them I'll kill myself." This so shocked Isaac that he sent for Jacob at once.

"Jacob, you are not to marry a Canaanite woman!"

"Father, I would never dream of marrying someone you did not choose."

"Go immediately to your mother's home in Haran and choose for yourself one of your uncle Laban's daughters. I give you permission to choose, and to negotiate the contract, and God bless your choice. And you are the right son to carry on the moral and spiritual inheritance of my father. You will certainly inherit this land." This was as close as he could come to admitting his error with Esau. Isaac embraced Jacob, and Rebecca held him close for a long time, reluctant to see him leave, but knowing that speed counted towards his safety. He would have to travel alone because he had missed the last caravan. Had she known that she would never see him again, she would not have had the strength to push him on his way.

"Goodbye, goodbye." She waved until he was just a speck in the distance, heading north.

Notes

The Biblical texts for this chapter are Genesis 24–27.

For background material, I recommend Oded Borowski, *Daily Life in Biblical Times* (Society of Biblical Literature, 2003); E. W. Barber, *Women's Work: the First 20,000 Years* (W. W. Norton, 1994); Carol L. Meyers, *Discovering Eve: Ancient Israelite Women in Context* (Oxford University Press, 1988). See especially Jennie Ebeling, *Women's Lives in Biblical Times* (T & T Clark International, 2010), chapters 2 and 4.

Rahel and Leah

"What a glorious day," thought Rahel as she walked alongside the flock of sheep, keeping them together by poking the strays with her long stick. "Come on, come on. We're almost at the well" she murmured aloud, humming a tune under her breath. "I'd rather be doing this than all the housework, any time. Who cares if it's dusty or if my feet and hands aren't soft, or that I'm sunburned. I'm free from any supervision and away from my father." She sang a line from the latest song that the wandering lute-player had entertained them with after supper on his way from Ur to Memphis. "Such wonderful stories. I wish I could travel to far-away places and see for myself the wonders of the world."

"Come on, little ones. The well is just over the hill. If we're late those rats of shepherds will put the boulder guarding the water back in place and you'll have nothing to drink."

In the distance she could see the gathering flocks, but squinting her eyes she thought that the boulder was still in place.

"Good. We have time yet. Even if they remove it now, they still have to water their own flocks. By the time we get there they will have finished and I will have just enough time to raise the water and pour it into the troughs for all of you. Far be it for any one of them to help me. He would be teased to death by the others. Why are men so silly? Too bad Tamar got married and had to stop working the flocks; I have no one to chat with any more." Rahel slowly made her way up and over the last hill with the baa-ing flock.

As Rahel neared the well, she looked up from the sheep and found herself staring into the almost black eyes of the best looking man she had ever seen. It was as though a flash of lightening passed between the two of them. He blushed and turned quickly to the boulder on the well, walked over to it and moved it all by himself! The shepherds watched with dropped jaws because even when all of them worked together, it was hard to move it. Now he was lifting the water and filling the nearest troughs, elbowing them aside to make room for Rahel's flocks.

Before she knew it, the stranger rushed over to her and kissed her on the cheek, stopping just as suddenly, and, of all things, crying out loud. She was about to run away from the madman, when he stopped her by speaking:

"Sorry, I'm so sorry. I know who you are but you do not know who I am. I am your father's sister's son. Rebecca's son from Canaan. We are cousins." His sentences were choppy, but his voice was most pleasing, and Rahel was elated. Looking him over again from under her lowered lashes she remarked on his powerful body, and guessed that under the traveler's dust was black hair and beard. But why was he alone? Had he traveled that dangerous route by himself?

"Can you herd the flock to Haran? Just walk within seeing distance of the other flocks and they will guide you," she said. "I will go ahead and inform my father of your arrival. He will be so pleased!" "So pleased my foot," she thought. Not if you came empty handed. Father never stops salivating over the story of how his sister's brideswealth was so rich. And so sudden. Abraham's slave arrived like a desert storm, whirling in and then away with aunt Rebecca." Thoughts of all sorts went through her mind as she hurried home. "This is my desert storm, my thunderbolt. I just know it!"

"Father, father! Where are you?" shouted Rahel, the excitement in her voice bringing not only her father, but her sister, mother, the secondary wives, and some of the slaves into the main part of the family compound.

"Where are the sheep? Why are you back so early? Has there been an accident?"

"No, only a miracle," Rahel gasped out trying to catch her breath.

"What are you saying? Speak clearly," commanded her father.

Rahel told of Jacob's arrival, omitting only her feelings for him. Her sister Leah eyed her closely, however, and knew that there was something more. Her father was already giving orders to clean out a guest room in the men's area, and telling his wife that he was going to have a lamb slaughtered for the evening meal in honor of his guest, rushed out of the house.

Leah, waiting until everyone had returned to their labor, approached her sister who was gulping down water in the eating area.

"Aren't you going to describe him to me?" Leah asked. "Or do you want him for yourself?"

"What are you talking about?" snapped Rahel, hating herself for blushing. "He's just a new-found cousin from Canaan. As interesting one, for a change, in this boring household."

"This is me you're talking to, dear sister. I can read you like a book. What does he look like? Is he the older twin or the younger one?"

"What difference does it make?" snapped Rahel again.

"To me it does," said Leah sweetly. "After all, it would be only fair if I had the older twin, since I'm older, and you have the younger."

"You don't even know if Jacob has come for a wife. He may just be here to visit us."

"Nonsense. No one comes just to visit. But if you won't tell me I'll see for myself shortly," Leah added, heading for the room she shared with Rahel.

"Where are you going?" asked Rahel, heading in that direction herself.

"To the chamber," replied Leah, entering ahead of Rahel and grabbing the small mirror to check on her hair. Rahel grabbed it out of her hands and held it up to her own face. Her hair had been covered when she left in the morning, but in her rush home, the kerchief had fallen off and curly damp tendrils went every which way around her face.

"Blasted hair," she mumbled, trying to flatten it down as her sister put a drop of kohl on her upper eyelid to enhance her already large dark eyes.

"Kohl? You are using kohl for a man you haven't even met," observed Rahel in astonishment.

"One can never tell about the future. I always like to be prepared," Leah answered passively.

They both heard the front gate open, and their father's voice.

"Welcome, nephew. Come in. That is quite a tale you tell. I am glad that my sister is well but sorry that your father is not. Girls, come greet your cousin Jacob who comes alone, with nothing but his bare hands," Laban said.

Rahel recognized her father's disappointment and was glad, because she despised his avarice. Leah was introduced, and Jacob politely greeted her, but his eyes moved immediately to Rahel, who felt an enormous surge of happiness course through her. Leah looked at her, then at him, and back again, sighing softly.

"Are you the older twin?" Leah asked.

"No," replied Jacob, "but I have the first-born's blessing."

All were shocked to hear this, so, over supper, Jacob told the family of the past week's events and why he had to flee Esau's wrath.

"I should hear from mother within the month," he concluded, but, having recognized his uncle's character already and remembering his mother's childhood stores about Laban, "don't worry, uncle. I won't eat you out of house and home. I have been well taught the arts of animal husbandry as well as the running of a huge household. I will work for my food."

"No, no," responded Laban with good Middle Eastern manners, but in his heart he was saying, "Yes, yes, a strong pair of hands that I can trust."

A month passed with no word from Canaan. Jacob questioned every caravan arriving in Haran, but there was nothing.

At supper, Laban—urged on by his family—asked his nephew directly: "Jacob, it is not right that you work this hard for no wages. Tell me what I should pay you and we will work out a deal."

Hovering nearby, Rahel held her breath. She and Jacob had discussed this topic when out of the hearing of the family compound. He had gradually taken over the care of the flocks, but she had gone with him many times to point out the pastures and the lie of the land. There was no question in her mind of the love she felt for Jacob.

"My uncle. I came empty-handed, but I came on my father's orders to arrange my own marriage with one of your daughters. My father delegated to me to negotiate my own brideswealth. I propose to work seven years for you as the brideswealth for your younger daughter Rahel."

"There, it was out. Now what would father say?" thought Rahel.

"Well, well. So it's Rahel that you want. I couldn't have guessed it," chuckled Laban aloud. Work in exchange for brideswealth." His mind was already calculating the value and he knew it was a great deal for him. "Done! Son-in-law to be! Let us draw up the betrothal contract and celebrate with my friends. Out, Rahel, as of tonight you are to wear the veil of betrothal in front of Jacob."

Rahel grabbed Leah and hugged her. Leah tried to be happy for Rahel, but it was difficult when she was feeling so sorry for herself. "What about me?" she thought. "When will my husband-to-be appear? Why does she have all the luck?" Tears filled her large beautiful eyes, but Rahel thought they were tears of shared joy, not envy.

The seven years flew by, so in love were Rahel and Jacob. They counted the seasons and marked them off. What they did not notice was the deepening melancholy of Leah. She cried constantly. Laban was beside himself. No word came from Canaan, and therefore the possibility of arranging a proper cousin marriage with Esau was disappearing. He had one daughter floating on air and one in the depths of depression. What to do? Cunningly he hit on a solution. "Yes, knowing as I do now, with his honor and his morals, it will work," he told himself. "Now the problem is how to deal with Rahel…"

"Uncle!" said Jacob. "The seven years are up. Please arrange for the completion of my marriage to Rahel."

"Certainly. We'll make the feast in two days' time. The women have to have time to prepare the food and the bride," responded Laban, his mind working quickly, refining his plan.

The next day, after Jacob left with the flocks, Laban sent a slave around to invite all the town leaders to the festivities. The rest of the household, under his wife's direction, busily prepared what could be prepared in advance. The compound was cleaned and the best carpets put out. The corner rooms were prepared for the bridal couple, allowing it a modicum of privacy in a society in which privacy was a luxury. Rahel supervised the decorations of her rooms, and set out her bridal robe. "Finally," she thought, 'I'll be rid of this betrothal veil."

"Be happy for me Leah," she cajoled her sister. "Please, it's my marriage night!" Leah tried to put on a smile, but was not quite successful.

43

The Biblical Woman

The pungent odor of roasting meat filled the compound. Fruit of all sorts were being piled up on the large copper trays, including huge sweet dates from Jericho. Breads by the hundreds were being baked; small sweet pancakes were frying. Young slaves were brushing away the flies. Others were squeezing oranges into ewers. One slave had the job a shelling a mountain of pistachio nuts.

Rahel was finished bathing and the slaves were dressing her hair; it was already mid-afternoon and the guests would be arriving at sunset. Laban entered the room dragging Leah in by the hand.

"Out," he ordered all the slaves. Rahel, startled, turned to face her father. One look at him and she knew that something awful was about to happen. Drawing himself up to his full height, he faced his daughter and declared: "You will not marry Jacob tonight. Leah will. There is no one proper and acceptable for her to marry, so I have decided that you will both marry Jacob. Close your mouth Rahel, and for heaven's sake Leah, stop your sniveling. I am your father, I am the patriarch, and I control all of your lives!"

"Father," gasped Rahel in horror, "You made a contract! Jacob will recognize it's not me! You will shame us all!"

"No," responded her father. "I've given this great thought. First, the two of you may have different faces and hair color but your shapes are the same and your voices similar. The bride will wear a thick veil, and a headpiece that will cover all her hair. She will speak only in a whisper, as is appropriate for a bride. Jacob, in his trust and simplicity, will never suspect a switch. I will also ply him with wine. It will be night and the bridal rooms are dark. In the dark one woman is just like another," Laban maliciously concluded.

Both sister started crying in earnest, realizing that their father's plan would work.

"Stop is, both of you, or I'll beat you up! I demand obedience!" Calling the slaves in, he directed them to dress a reluctant Leah in the bridal robe. Rahel, stiffly moving to the divan, felt her life moving out of control. She sat immobile as the sun set and Leah was led out of their shared room into the public part of the compound. The sound of music and laughter and talk drifted in to her, but she could not move. "Jacob," she wept to herself, for there were no more tears left. "Jacob, it's not me, it's not me."

She was still on the divan early the next morning when she heard a great shout from the far side of the house. She heard Jacob's anguished voice shouting at her father.

"What did you do? How dare you switch daughters? I will bring you to justice for breaking our contract! Where is my Rahel? Why did you trick me?" The veins of his forehead were protruding, and Laban knew that he had better be careful for in his anger Jacob had both the physical power and the possibility of killing him.

"It is not done in Haran to marry off the younger before the elder," began Laban in a reasonable tone. Jacob grabbed his shepherd's crook and started for Laban. Stepping backward, he kept his tone reasonable and continued, "Now, Jacob, you already cohabited with Leah. You don't want to shame her, do you? Let us finish the week of celebrating her marriage, and on the eighth day you can marry Rahel." Jacob hesitated. Pushing his advantage, Laban daringly continued, "of course that would mean seven more years of labor for Leah's brideswealth, but, but…" as Jacob's face darkened again, "not seven more years of waiting. Just seven more days."

Jacob saw Rahel at the doorway of her room, and overcome with anguish for her predicament, as well as sympathy for Leah who was shaking in the doorway of the new rooms, Jacob gave in. Triumphantly Laban reached out to embrace his son-in-law, but that was too much for Jacob, whose face reflected how much he despised Laban and held him in contempt.

Rahel stayed in her room for the entire week of Leah's marriage festivities. By the time it was her turn to be led to the marriage ceremony, she had accepted the fact that she and Leah were to be co-wives of equal status and with equal access to their husband. But she knew that Jacob loved her, and her alone. That is what gave her the strength to carry on.

The compound had to be rearranged, for co-wives had to be treated equally. Therefore, Leah had a room at the far end of the rectangle, then there was a neutral room, then Rahel's room. As was usual, meals were eaten with the rest of the extended family. Normally the wife moved into her husband's extended family structure, but there were instances of matrilocal arrangements as well. In this case, since Jacob could not go back to Canaan, he lived with his father-in-law, worked with him, and owed him obedience. Jacob chafed at the situation, but until he worked off Leah's brideswealth, he was stuck, for he was an honorable man, and his word counted.

Rahel pretended that Leah was not there. She avoided her as much as possible, and rarely spoke to her father, whom she now despised with her entire being. The more she learned from Jacob about his God, the more decadent and infantile the town's polytheism seemed. They had nothing to do with the fertility festivals nor with the harvest festivities. Nothing Laban could do would change Jacob's mind on this one issue.

Jacob spent all his nights with Rahel, also barely acknowledging Leah's existence. But Leah, smiling to herself, went about her business, until one day, over four months after their marriages, Rahel noticed her sister's protuberant belly.

"You're pregnant!" she gasped, trying to control her envy.

"That's right, my sister. You may have Jacob's love, but I will bear Jacob his first child. Hopefully it will be a boy. Then who will he love more? The mother of his son or a childless wife?"

Jacob had mixed feelings upon being informed of his impending fatherhood. He really did not like Leah, though he was kind to her. And that personal slave of hers that she received as her father's wedding gift, Zilpa, was always fussing over her. Why could she not be more like Rahel's personal slave, Bilha. What a house of women!

Rahel worked hard on controlling her envy of Leah, but when the child was born and it was a boy, she feared for her place in Jacob's heart. Leah triumphantly named her son Reuben, showing off at the naming ceremony that God saw her suffering, and sent her a son for now her husband would love her.

Rahel need not have worried for Jacob still loved her. However he did cohabit with Leah after she had recovered from childbirth, as was her right. A few months after that, Rahel passed Leah in the courtyard where she was playing with the baby. With a start Rahel realized that her sister was pregnant again.

"No," she cried to herself. Leah sat there with a very self-satisfied look on her face, knowing how anguished Rahel was over her own infertility. A second boy was born, but at the naming Leah showed her own less than perfect situation for she called the child Simon, because God had seen that she was hated and thus had given her a second son. Then came a third one, and again Leah's misery was openly proclaimed for when she named the newborn Levi she said it was because this time her husband will live with her after bearing him three sons. But it did not happen, and at the birth of her fourth son, Leah's name of Judah showed her acceptance of her situation, in merely blessing God for a healthy child.

With each birth, Rahel grew more and more nervous. "What is the matter with me? Why can't I conceive?" Jacob tried to calm her by telling her of the long years that his mother had waited, and the even longer years that his grandmother Sara had waited. After much anguish and contemplation, Rahel decided to emulate Sara.

"If I don't have children I may as well be dead," Rahel told Jacob, knowing full well what his reaction would be.

"Am I God who kept you from being pregnant?" shouted a frustrated Jacob.

"Jacob, this is very hard for me, so please let me speak my piece. I want you to take Bilha as a secondary wife—like your grandmother did with Hagar—and I will adopt Bilha's child. Perhaps after this adoption I may even be able to have a child of my own."

Jacob looked at her beautiful but pained face. He sympathized totally with her and knew that offering her slave Bilha to him was an act of desperation. How could he refuse his beloved wife anything? Besides, as a matriarch it was her right to have a slave bear a child for her. No one, of course, asked for Bilha's approval.

With mixed feelings on the part of everyone except Bilha, who was only too glad to be a secondary wife to such a handsome and kind patriarch, the marriage took place. Laban had no say because Bilha would not be challenging his daughter's superior status. Leah had no say because she already had four sons.

Bilha became pregnant at once, again to Rahel's mixed feelings. But Rahel was going to stick to her decision, and when the baby arrived,

Rahel—as Bilha's mistress, and as an act of adoption—named him Dan because God had judged her, listened to her plea, and sent her a son. But one was not enough for Rahel, looking at her sister's boisterous flock. So Bilha cohabited again with Jacob, and soon a second son was born, and again Rahel named him. Naphtali was chosen as the name, to signify that in her competition with her sister, she, Rahel, had prevailed with this second adoption.

When Leah realized that her own fertility had ceased, she demanded equal treatment with her personal slave, Zilpa. Jacob had no say, but was not very happy to have to take another secondary wife. Zilpa became pregnant immediately, and at the birth of her first son, Leah named him Gad, and immediately demanded a second cohabitation. Zilpa then gave birth to a second son, and Leah named him Asher.

Eight sons in as many years. Jacob was certainly prospering. He had also worked out an agreement with his chameleon-like father-in-law with regard to his labor in exchange for newborn animals. Laban kept changing the terms of the agreement, but Jacob had learned how to deal with him, and with God's help, his own personal flocks had grown. He was becoming moderately rich. Now if only he could go home.

Reuben, a strapping boy of ten, went out in the fields during the spring wheat harvest. He had some free time to explore alone, away from all the noise of the family compound. He espied some mandrakes hidden among the rocks near the crops. Mandrakes! He carefully dug up the plants, roots and all, knowing that his mother—and all women—made love potions from the fruit, aphrodisiacs from the leaves, and love charms from the twisted roots. His mother could certainly use all the help she could get to lure his father away from Aunt Rahel.

Reuben entered the compound heading for his mother's rooms, carrying the mandrakes carefully. But Rahel saw what he was holding, and followed him into Leah's room.

"Give me, please, your son's mandrakes," Rahel asked Leah.

Leah lashed out, surprising even herself with her vindictiveness. "Isn't it enough that you have taken my husband? Why do you also want my son's mandrakes?"

Startled, Rahel rose to the bait. "All right. I'll pay for them. I'll trade you my night with Jacob tonight for the mandrakes."

"Accepted," crowed Leah. Reuben disappeared thinking that he would never ever take more than one wife.

That evening, as Jacob returned with the flocks, he was surprised to be met by Leah. Seeing his questioning look, Leah said: "You are to come to me tonight for I traded this night with you for my son's mandrakes." "I wonder how other men deal with co-wives," thought Jacob as he glumly followed an exuberant Leah into her room.

Nine months later, there was a new arrival in the busy household. Leah named this son Issachar, explaining the God rewarded her for unselfishly giving Zilpa to Jacob as a secondary wife. Another son arrived nearly a year later, and Leah name him Zebulon, explaining, "God has given me a godly gift: now my husband will live with me, for I have given him six sons." A year later, Leah gave birth once more, to the first girl of the household. She named her Dina, and she was pampered and fussed over by all her brothers who were fascinated by her femininity.

Rahel, watching her sister give birth year after year, felt herself gradually relax into acceptance of her childlessness. She played with her two adopted sons and matured into a true matriarchal figure. Leah, so busy with her many children, gladly left most of the running of the growing household to Rahel. She had accepted God's will, and even Jacob remarked on how peaceful and happy she had become. Therefore when the first signs of pregnancy appeared Rahel paid no attention to them, thinking that she had indigestion, and then that she was getting fat. It wasn't until she was in her fourth or fifth month, while she was bending over to correct a new slave's weaving, that she felt a flutter in her belly. Her heart in her mouth, she slowly stood up. The flutter repeated itself. Leah walked by just then, and seeing her sister's astonished look, asked if she was all right.

"Is it like a butterfly's wings?" Rahel softly asked.

"What?" Then Leah saw that Rahel's hands were on her enlarged belly. "Rahel, Rahel. You're pregnant!" Even Leah was ecstatic over the news, which immediately spread through the household. Even Laban, who rarely came to Jacob's quarters, stopped by to wish her good luck. As for Jacob, no words could express his joy.

Rahel thought of boy's names and girl's names, but when the baby was born and she held him for the first time, all she could think of was her desire for another baby. So she named him Joseph, so that God would add another baby. Everyone who came to visit remarked on the resemblance of Joseph to Rahel, and Jacob, despite Rahel's warnings, showed his preference for Joseph over all his other sons right from the beginning.

"My husband, be careful of favoritism. You yourself suffered from it as a child when your father preferred Esau over you."

"I can't help it, Rahel. He looks just like you, beautiful all over!"

"The other boys resent him already, especially Simon and Levi. I always have to be alert when they play with him because their "play" ends up each time with Joseph crying. They really are quite a twosome. Simon is already incredibly powerful."

"Yes. He reminds me of my brother, but I am trying to channel his power into labor. He already has major responsibilities with the flocks. My six-year arrangement with your father is almost up and God has blessed me with many healthy newborn animals. What a snake that man is, constantly changing the wording of the agreement. Well, this time it didn't work for him, and we will leave for Canaan as soon as God orders me to go."

"How can we? My father considers you his good luck charm, because it is your skill with the flocks that has made him rich."

"We will wait until the shearing season when he and your brothers will be in the far pastures…"

"Shh. Someone may hear. The walls have ears."

Some time later, Reuben came casually into the compound. Walking into his mother's room, he told a startled Leah that Jacob wanted to see her immediately in the southern pasture. He then told Rahel the same thing. The two women asked no questions, covered their hair against the dust, put on their heavy sandals, and followed Reuben. On the way, Rahel told Leah what it may be about, and when they met their husband with no spying eyes and ears around them, Jacob informed them that God had given him his long-anticipated order. But, since their marriage contracts had been matrilocal, and Laban held the capital of their brideswealth, he needed their official permission to move away from their father's home, possibly at the loss of their own personal wealth. Jacob added that Laban's attitude towards him had changed over the past six years as Jacob's flocks had flourished and Laban's had just had average growth.

Rahel and Leah began to speak at the same time. Leah deferred to Rahel, who stated firmly, "Jacob, you may not realize that our father has not only used the interest of our brideswealth, but has also spent the capital. I know this because I run the entire household now that our mother has died. We have no share in our father's household and no inheritance. We are considered strangers by him and useless, since he has used up everything."

Leah added: "If your flocks have been flourishing at the expense of our father's, it is God's way of paying us back what legally belongs to us. We both agree to follow you and move to Canaan." Rahel nodded.

"Fine, but we have to act quickly, for tomorrow Laban leaves for the farthest, northern pasture. It will take him three days to get there, which will give us one week's head start traveling south. I pray that it is enough."

The women returned to Haran, excitedly planning out their move, what to take and what to leave.

"Finally we will leave this heathen city and head out for the hills and the free semi-nomadic life of Jacob's parents."

Laban and his sons left at sunrise. Jacob brought his camels into the compound opening, and Rahel directed their loading. The oldest boys were in charge of the flocks, waiting in the southern fields until Jacob would send word for them to head for the boundary of Haran's distant fields. In the midst of all the hubbub, Rahel sneaked into her father's rooms. "This is my last chance at some sort of revenge. I want him to suffer as he made me suffer. There they are."

She had a large colorful camel bag in her hands. Into it she stuffed Laban's *terafim* or household gods, ugly grinning creatures which were supposed to guard the luck of the household. Chuckling to herself,

Rahel pictured in her mind's eye how desperate Laban would be. He never went anywhere without patting them, or making small offerings of sweet things and wine before them. She loaded the bags over her camel and climbed up onto the saddle. Leah was already on hers, and Bilha and Zilpa on their camels. The youngest children rode with their mothers. The slaves followed on foot. Jacob gave the signal, the camels noisily arose, the gates were opened, and they were off, waving to their astonished neighbors. One of them would now take it upon himself to run to Laban to inform him of the unexpected news.

Moving as quickly as he could, with so many women and young children, Jacob led the way across the river towards Mount Gilead, which they reached in a week's time. Setting up camp on the mountain side, they saw the dust storm from the north announcing the imminent arrival of a fast-moving group. They all knew that it must be Laban and his men.

Jacob motioned to his wives to go to their individual tents. "This is my affair, this is my land, and although I fear your father, I will fight for our freedom. God will protect us." Rahel and Leah moved away, Rahel's mind racing, trying to figure out how to cover up her theft of the *terafim*. She knew that although Jacob despised polytheism, he would never steal, not even household gods. She could hear her father shouting, accusing, twisting things around, as if he really would have sent them off willingly. He would have kept them all enslaved to him forever. Now she heard the voices nearing the tents. She guessed that her father was searching for the *terafim*, first in Jacob's tent, then Leah's to the left, then the shared tent of Bilha and Zilpa behind Jacob's. "Here he comes," Rahel thought.

Laban furiously pushed open Rahel's tent flap, his small black eyes darting all over.

"Forgive me Father for not rising in your presence, for the way of women is upon me and I am in great pain," Rahel said sweetly, inclining her head towards Laban in a sign of filial respect.

Laban grunted, as he poked into everything but did not find what he was searching for. He left the tent without so much as a word, leaving Rahel to quietly pat the camel bag on which she was sitting. "That is one time that the taboo on touching a menstruating woman paid off in favor of a woman." She laughed to herself. "He didn't even look at me. I hope I never see him again."

Rahel arose and stood outside her tent. She could see that the other women had done the same. Now she heard Jacob's voice raised in anger. Rahel knew that this was only a ploy to fight Laban with his own weapon, namely play acting. But once Jacob started, the twenty years of bottled up complaints bubbled over. The more he shouted, stepping forward each time, closer and closer to Laban, the quieter Laban got and the more thoughtful. In a conciliatory tone, and fearful of Jacob's God, Laban actually did something to atone a little for his past behavior.

"Let us make a pact, Jacob. Let us gather these stones to serve as a witness that you swear that you will not take any further wives, lest you spoil the inheritance of my grandchildren. Normally I would have had this written on parchment, witnessed, signed and sealed. But we are in the wilderness, so that your word will have to be enough, with the God of Abraham and the god of Nahor as our guarantors."

Jacob readily agreed, and made an offering on the stones. They all then sat to await the preparation of supper. After eating, everyone but Jacob went to sleep, for he did not trust Laban at all. But with sunrise, Laban arose, ate with his men, and called for his daughters and grandchildren.

"Farewell, may God bless you all," he said as he kissed each grandchild. He embraced Leah, but did not touch Rahel, which was just as well for her. The thought of his embrace made her sick to her stomach. He was gone. She would never have to see him again.

The camp broke up, the animals were loaded, and they were on their way again. But now that the danger with Laban was over, they still had to face the danger of Esau. Jacob sent messengers to inform his brother of his arrival in Canaan as Jacob's tactics were worked out: better a confrontation than living in constant fear. The messengers returned to state that Esau was coming to greet him with four hundred men.

Jacob's heart fell, and with great trepidation, he continued with his plan. The camp and flocks were divided into two groups so that at least one could escape should Esau attack. Then he prayed to God for strength, as he chose three groups of animals from his flocks to send as gifts to his brother. He then took his co-wives and secondary wives and all his children, helping them cross the Yabok river, recrossing to spend the night alone with the larger portion of his flocks and slaves.

Later Jacob told Rahel of his experience in wrestling with a strange man until dawn, and how the man had injured his thigh before Jacob realized he was God's messenger. Jacob had held on, refusing to free the man until he received a blessing. The blessing included a new name, Israel. Limping, Jacob crossed the river, reinvigorated in his belief in God to face Esau, who had arrived in a whirlwind of dust with sunrise.

Bilha and Zilpa and their sons went forward to bow before Esau and greet him. Esau was surprised at this, but politely accepted their greeting. Then came Leah surrounded by her six strapping sons; they too bowed before Esau. Again, he responded politely. "Jacob's ploy is working", thought Rahel, "he does not look angry anymore, but thoughtful. My turn." She took Joseph's hand and slowly approached her brother-in-law. "He looks like a wild man, but he also looks like Jacob, only his features are coarse whereas Jacob's are refined." She inclined her head, knowing that her posture informed Esau of her importance in the family. Joseph examined his uncle and grinned widely. Esau smiled back and rushed forward to embrace Jacob in a huge bear hug, and both men started to weep. Jacob wept partly from relief, but the danger was not yet over, for Esau's chameleon-like personality could just as easily change back to anger. He had not lived all those years with Laban not to have learned a few lessons in manipulation.

Rahel listened with delight as she recognized Jacob's ploy. "Please accept my gift, Esau."

"But it's too great, my brother. I have enough of my own."

"I insist, since God has blessed me so."

"All right, but we will escort you into Canaan."

"No, my brother. Your men move quickly and I have young children, young animals and women in my camp."

"Then I will just leave some men to guard you."

"I appreciate it but better not."

Esau and his men ate with the family, then they re-mounted their horses, and with a huge smile for all, Esau galloped off to his desert home.

Rahel walked up to her husband, stood very close and softly stated: "You did it Jacob. You succeeded with both my father and your brother. Let's continue to our new home in peace."

They moved slowly through the land, first settling near Shechem, where a most shameful thing happened, namely the rape of Dina, then near Bethel, where God renewed his covenant with Jacob as the spiritual heir of Abraham and Isaac. Canaan would be his.

Rahel was oblivious to the events, good and bad, occurring to the family. Her life centered on Joseph, Jacob, and her new pregnancy. It was more difficult this time as the family was constantly on the move, but Rahel felt good and enjoyed the internal tickling of the growing infant. Joseph was happy for his mother, but he wondered if the new baby would cause his father to divide his love and so he would not be the favorite any more.

They had just reached the outskirts of the town of Efrat when Rahel felt the labor pains begin. Jacob quickly gave orders to pitch the tents, and rushed in to see Rahel. The midwife was kneeling before her and Leah was holding her hands. The midwife's worried face told Jacob all. He refused to leave the birthing area, sponging Rahel's face with cool water. Finally the midwife reached into the womb and turned the baby over. He burst out in a gush of liquid, and the midwife cheered Rahel by saying, "Look, this one too is a boy!"

Rahel looked at him, smiled weakly and sadly, saying that he should be named "Ben-Oni", the son of my travail.

Joseph was rushed into the tent. Rahel embraced him and said, "Be a good boy Joseph, don't be vain, and take care of your little brother. Remember that I love you." A bewildered Joseph went over to look at the newborn, as his father embraced his mother whispering endearments. Then Joseph heard a sound that would give him nightmares for the rest of his life: his father crying in anguish. Rahel had died.

When his racking sobs at last ceased, Leah gently removed his grip, saying that he had to leave, for Rahel's body had to be prepared for burial. "Will we take her to Hebron, to the double cave?"

"No," whispered Jacob. "Let us bury her here along the main road. She can be a protector to all travellers this way. Where are we, anyway?"

"Bethlehem," said Leah.

The next morning the grave was dug and Rahel was buried. While Jacob busied himself with erecting a stone marker on the grave, the infant Benjamin was given to the care of a wetnurse, a slave whose infant had died the day before. Leah now directed the huge women's world along, missing her sister more than she could have imagined.

"Yes, I wanted Jacob to myself, but not at this price," she thought as she watched her sons reach maturity. "I guess one has to be careful of what one wishes for, because the wish can come true. I certainly could use Rahel to help with the complicated problems of this family, starting with Jacob's favoritism for Joseph, continuing through the horror of Dina's attack, and then the constant bickering of the boys. Funny, how I still think of them as boys when half of them are already married. And what an array of daughters-in-law I now have to supervise! God give me strength."

Notes

The Biblical texts for this chapter are Genesis 27–32, 35.

For background material, I recommend Morris Silver, *Prophets and Markets: The Political Economy of Ancient Israel* (Kluwer Academic Publishing, 1982); Philip J. King and Lawrence Stager, *Life in Biblical Israel* (John Knox Press, 2001). See especially Jennie R. Ebeling, *Women's Lives in Biblical Times* (T & T Clark International, 2010), chapters 4 and 5.

Powerless Women: Dina and Tamar

As the family and flocks slowly made their way south from Haran into Canaan, Dina observed the countryside gradually change. She had seen her first rivers, real rivers, not just streams for washing and drinking. She also had seen her first huge snow-capped mountain far off in the distance. Traveling was so much more exciting than living in the confined women's quarters in Haran. Why, she couldn't even go out with the flocks, as her aunt Rahel had done, because she had eleven brothers to share out that work. Boys had all the fun jobs and adventures. All she had to look forward to was marriage. She wondered for the hundredth time if her father would arrange a cousin-marriage for her with one of uncle Esau's sons. She didn't think so, after seeing for herself what kind of wild man he was. She also knew that he was not as God-fearing as her father would want.

Dina slid down the side of her camel and joined her older brothers with the flocks.

"And what do you want, little pest?" teased Reuben.

"Decent conversation, if you please," Dina primly replied.

"When you do that with your face you look just like mother," said Simon giving her a push.

"Is that good or bad?" asked Dina

They only laughed.

"Do I look like mother?" she asked Judah. He observed her closely and said: "you have her luminous brown eyes, but the rest of your face is like grandfather's, without a beard."

"I don't want to look like him. I don't like him," she pouted.

"Spoiled little girl," Levi added his two cents.

"I am not. I'm not spoiled and I'm not a little girl. Fourteen is marriage age for a girl, as you will know. You will all miss me after I'm married off," she huffed.

"Well, if you want to make a good match, you had better not get blisters on your dainty feet from walking with us," said Naphtali.

"Who asked you, you slave's son?" snapped Dina.

"Unfair, unfair," interrupted Reuben. "We're all father's children and there is no favoritism."

"What?" Simon said. "No favoritism? And what do you call father's behavior with golden boy Joseph?"

They all fell silent thinking about the unfairness of life.

"The first thing I'm going to do when we reach a settled area is find some girlfriends," stated Dina, changing the topic. "I need some female company my own age."

"Why, mother and aunt Rahel, and Bilha and Zilpa aren't enough for you?" Levi asked, teasingly.

"I said my own age. What a family. So many women in one generation and so many men in the next," she complained. "No one understands me."

"Oh, oh, oh," all the brothers moaned in chorus.

Dina laughed, swatting her biggest and most favorite brother, Simon, who merely picked her up and carried her across his shoulders as he would a lame sheep.

"Put me down, you barbarian. You sometimes remind me of Uncle Esau!" Simon put her down and patted her affectionately on the head with his enormous hand messing up her kerchief and her hair.

"There is father giving the signal to stop for the night. Bye to all. It's time for me to turn into a bread baker or water pourer or baby minder, depending on what mother thinks up for me this afternoon." She turned back to her camel, scaled up its side before Leah could see that she had been walking, and innocently allowed herself to be led off to the women's area.

"Dina, the pieces of squash must be cut smaller or they will not cook on time," Leah said overseeing her daughter's work.

"If I make them smaller I may cut my fingers," she responded.

"Not if you are careful and do it the way I showed you."

"Why should I learn this anyway? I'll always have slaves for this work," Dina complained.

Powerless Women: Dina and Tamar

"You don't know that as a fact, number one. Number two, in order to supervise, you have to know how to do it yourself."

"All right, mother. I hear you. There, is that better?"

Just then Rahel walked over to check up on the food preparations.

"Good work, Dina," she said, smiling at her niece.

Dina unwillingly found herself smiling back. She was very protective of her mother and understood the undercurrents of love-hate-envy of the two co-wives, but with aunt Rahel so radiant in her new pregnancy, she could not be nasty to her.

"Do you know where we are, aunt Rahel?" Dina asked.

"I think that we are a day or two away from a city-state called Shechem. It is in the midst of a huge fertile valley, and is similar to Haran, or so your father claims. He visited there ages ago when he lived with his parents."

The food was finally ready, and the slaves brought it out to the men. She and the women sat in the women's area eating their supper. Babies and toddlers crawled or ran around, free at last after a long day in the baskets on the camels.

"This is the life," sighed Dina looking up at the stars. "I'm so happy now."

The next day, there was an anticipating feeling in the moving group, that they would be able to settle down for a while. Jacob intended to buy a piece of land for them to set up with tents, and there was excellent pasturage for the flocks. Dina could make out the walled city in the distance, and she happily made plans to go looking for girlfriends as soon as she could get away from the campsite. Perhaps the young women met at the main well just as they did in Haran.

Adjusting her hair covering to protect herself from the dust, Dina started out for the city. She knew from her father that Canaan was made up of a series of city-states in pacts of mutual protection one with the other. That way if one city was attacked, other contracting cities would help it out and expect the same in return.

"Where are you going, Dina?" asked her brother Zebulon, who was only a year older than her. "Should I come with you?"

"Go away. Now. I finally got away and you had to follow me. I'm going to Shechem to make friends with young women my own age.

I don't need a guard. Go." Dina overwhelmed him, and as usual Zebulon gave in, watching with mixed feelings as his sister crossed the field in the direction of a small growth of trees.

Dina soon reached the trees, and, as it had started to get hot she decided to rest a bit in the shade. She did not notice a movement in the shadow, and even if she had, she would have felt no fear because Haran was an open society in which women could go around alone without fear of molestation. That was the only society that Dina knew. She could not imagine that Canaan would be different.

There was even a small bubbling spring inside the copse, and Dina knelt to cup her hands and drink. She sensed a movement behind her and spun around fearing a wild animal but it was only a young man.

"Well, well. What have we here? A beautiful strange damsel alone and unafraid?" he questioned in his strangely accented Aramaic. "How about a kiss, lovely lady?"

"No. Thank you, no. I'll be going now," Dina replied, feeling very uncomfortable but not knowing why.

"You can't be that innocent. No Canaanite woman is," the man continued looking her over, and moving closer.

"I'm not Canaanite but Hebrew. My father is Jacob and…"

"And I am prince of the city. I do what I want and there is no one to stop me. If I tell you to kiss me that is what you do!"

"I take orders from no one except my father," retorted Dina, and with a feint that usually worked with her brothers, she tried to run past this nasty stranger. But he caught her robe and she rushed away and held on tightly. She lost her balance and when she fell, her robe moved displaying a long length of bare legs. Since she was on her stomach she could not see the facial expression of her tormentor, which was probably just as well, for the next few minutes were branded in her memory forever. Her attacker overpowered her, pulled her robe over her head and raped her.

Dina was in shock. Nothing had prepared her for the pain, anguish and shame that she felt.

"Now, wasn't that fun?" said her attacker, as he turned her over and pulled her robe back into place. Startled at her facial expression, he looked down at himself and realized at once that she had never been with a man before.

She started to shake, a trembling that would not stop. The princeling reached out to hold her, a strange feeling creeping up on him as he patted her head awkwardly. "Why do I feel that I have to protect you? Why do I feel guilty? I've never felt guilty about anything in my life"

Dina's teeth were chattering as she went into deep shock. The princeling lifted her up and carried her into Shechem, into his father's house, into the women's quarters.

"Mother, take care of this young woman, but also make sure that she can't get out," he ordered the matriarch.

"Father," he said to Hamor, "go to the Hebrew campsite and negotiate a marriage agreement for me with their daughter." Startled, Hamor opened his mouth, but after on look at his determined son, set out for Jacob's campsite. "And I'm coming too."

"Where is Dina?" asked Leah, "it's time to prepare supper." No one had seen her. Zebulon reluctantly came forward and told his mother where he had seen her. Jacob immediately set out with Zebulon to check out what happened to his daughter. When they reached the copse of trees, they searched and found Dina's headscarf caught on one of the low bushes.

"Father," said Zebulon, "it looks like there was a fight here. Look, here is a tuft of fabric that is the color of Dina's robe. Father, what could have happened?"

Jacob feared for the worst, remembering clearly the immorality of the Canaanites, but since his older sons were out with the flocks, he would have to await their return before acting. He returned slowly to the campsite, to arrive only minutes before Hamor.

Jacob greeted Hamor and Shechem in the public area of his largest tent. Hamor entered and sat alongside his son and the men examined each other while water was brought and some mint tea. Hamor then cleared his throat, introduced himself and his son and told a panicking Jacob that his son Shechem, princeling of the city Shechem, wanted to marry his daughter.

"How is it that your son knows of my daughter?" began Jacob ignoring the princeling.

"It seems that he met her in the fields," said Hamor, refusing to meet Jacob's eyes.

"He met her in the fields and immediately wants to marry her?" continued Jacob, looking directly at Shechem. "What kind of meeting was it?"

"I'm not sure. All I know is that he is in love with your daughter."

"Where is my daughter?" asked Jacob, his voice rising. He heard the sounds of men's excited voices in the clearing. Reuben, Simon, and Levi rushed into the tent, all shouting at once, the other sons on their heels.

"Father, something horrible happened to Dina!" They stopped short on seeing Hamor and Shechem and, remembering their manners, closed their mouths.

Jacob introduced his sons to Hamor and his son, who, sizing them up, was very impressed. He was even more impressed with the size of Jacob's flocks, as well as with the rich trappings inside the tent. Addressing all of them, Hamor stated that his son, the princeling Shechem, wanted to marry their sister. "He is mad about her and his soul desires her as his wife. Marry your daughter to us and you marry our daughters, and you can live peacefully in our land, trade in it, and own parts of it."

Hamor offered Jacob the most important thing a semi-nomad could want: the right to settle, along with protection. He did not do this out of generosity, but out of a calculation of Jacob's wealth and the need to keep the peace. But Shechem, in his self-centeredness and indifference to protocol burst out: "Whatever you desire as bridesweatlh, I will give. Name your price and I will meet it, only agree to let me marry the young woman."

Jacob's sons were seething because they had already heard that Shechem had raped Dina. But they did not act impetuously because they knew that the army of the city-state outnumbered them, and that Dina was being held inside the walls. Judah, the most rational of the sons said politely: "We cannot intermarry, for uncircumcised men are taboo to us, and an abomination. The only condition that we ask is that you all become like us, circumcising all your men. Then we will give our daughters to you, and we will marry your young women, and we will become one people. If not, we will take our sister and go."

Father and son looked at each other, Shechem nodding slightly. Hamor concluded the marriage negotiations happily, and the two men left for the city, telling Jacob that they would fulfill the agreement and be ready for the marriage ceremony within the week.

"I can't believe it, Father. No wealth, no gems, no silver, just the short discomfort of circumcision. And then she'll be mine forever."

Hamor and Shechem discussed how to best present the proposal to the entire male population. After all, not all would profit directly from the deal. Shechem said he would use all of his wide influence on the young men by reporting how beautiful the women in Jacob's family were, while Hamor could address the older men and stress Jacob's wealth. By the time they reached the walls of Shechem, they knew exactly what each would say.

"When would we have to be circumcised?" asked one of the elders.

"Tomorrow," responded Shechem

"Boy, you really lust after her, don't you?" teased one of his friends. Shechem was not embarrassed. He knew that the whole city knew of the rape, but no one had dared reprimand him. They even admired him and now looked forward to sharing Jacob's wealth.

The next day all the males of Shechem were circumcised. They drank jugs of wine before the operation, and drunkenly survived the first two days. On the third day the pain penetrated their blunted sense and they lay moaning in pain in their homes, wondering why they had agreed to Hamor's plan.

Meanwhile Jacob's sons bided their time, seething in anger at the humiliation of their sister which shamed the entire family. Imagine, the city had not punished the princeling! It was unheard of anywhere that a rapist of a freeborn woman should not be punished.

Word came to them of the mass circumcision, and they waited for the third day when they knew that the pain would be incapacitating. They were all going to free Dina from Shechem's home. In the end, however, only two of the brothers went, revenge burning in their blood.

Simon and Levi took their short swords and hid them under the folds of their robes until actually inside the walls. They knew where Hamor's house was, and headed there, noting the groans from the houses that they passed. No men, and no boys were in the streets, not even the municipal guards.

Approaching their target, Levi pushed open the front door, and Simon slipped quickly inside. They quickly opened one door after the other in the compound. They heard voices in the far room.

"So, my beauty. Today is the painful crisis, but then I'll heal and we will marry. Please eat something. You haven't touched a morsel of food since…since you came here. Come on, the term of the marriage have been met and it was your brothers who set the terms."

"Don't touch me, you foul creature. My brothers will save me, not allow me to marry an immoral excuse for a man…" Dina looked up and saw Simon in the doorway. Shechem saw him too, and seeing the sword, tried to defend himself. With a roar, Simon lunged the sword through his body, bellowing: "Rapist! Defiler!" Grabbing Dina by the hand, Simon rushed back through the door where he met Levi, his sword dripping blood too.

"I got the father! Let's go!"

"Go? Go? I'm going to kill them all! They all are guilty for our shame because they didn't punish the rapist!" he said with clenched teeth. "Are you with me?"

Within the hour the two brothers killed every male in the city state. By that time the rest of the brothers arrived, the blood-revenge accepted by them, and they looted the entire place, enslaving all the women and children while loading up the goods and collecting the flocks. Finally, Jacob's sons returned with Dina to their father.

"Dina. Dina, my daughter."

"Father, what shall I do? My life is over."

"Shh, shh. You're home and your mother awaits you. You will heal and feel better with time." Leah gently led her into her tent, where the other women awaited to wash her and cuddle her and love her.

Jacob turned to his dusty sons, and noted the bloody swords hanging over Simon and Levi's robes. He stood at the opening of his tent and

Powerless Women: Dina and Tamar

saw the flocks and slaves and asses piled with goods. Slowly turning to Simon and Levi, he asked: "What happened? Leave nothing out."

After they finished, Jacob said: "What have you done? Don't you understand the political structure of city-states? Now all those in contract to protect Shechem will attack us, and we are vastly outnumbered. We will be destroyed!"

Simon replied: "Should we have allowed our sister to be treated as a harlot?"

That night God appeared to Jacob telling him to move the Bethel and build an altar there. The family moved the next day, and after a few nervous days of checking the horizon for the rising dust of an attacking army, Jacob realized that the Canaanites had accepted the blood revenge taken on Shechem as proper punishment for the actions of the men of the city-state as a whole.

The problem now was Dina. She looked like a shadow of herself. Leah said she didn't sleep at night, and if she did, had nightmares. The only one who seemed to bring out a shadow of a smile was that hulk of a son, Simon. Who would have thought he could be so gentle, when he was such a brutal and dangerous man.

Some time later, Leah approached Jacob, her face filled with concern.

"It's not over. I think our Dina is pregnant. I am afraid that when she realizes what is going on, she will kill herself."

"Let me think about it. Perhaps I'll discuss it with our sons."

"You are thinking of Simon, right? He has two wives, both expecting babies. Do you think that Dina would be happy living in his smaller household, sharing the care of three babies? It is an idea."

Simon accepted the responsibility for Dina, and spoke to her gently, yet insistently. No, she would not have to marry and move away. No, he was not shamed by her pregnancy for it was not her fault. No, he would not hate the baby because the baby was half hers. Yes, father and mother agreed that she would be more comfortable away from the main tents with the rivalries between Leah and Rahel and all the brothers. More private. Yes, he would protect her forever.

Dina finally agreed and moved into Simon's small but growing family, where she lived with his two wives who were her age. She liked them and gradually life's daily routines took over, and Dina drifted into history.

* * *

After the rape of Dina, and the death of Rahel, Jacob could not imagine that anything worse could happen. He knew he should not favor Joseph, but he couldn't help himself—the youth looked just like Rahel did when he had first met her. If only he were not so vain, especially with those dreams of his.

Another trauma hit the family. Joseph was sold into slavery by his brothers, who told their father that he had been killed by a wild animal. Then Judah, without saying a word, walked out on the family to start his own patriarchy. He did not even ask Jacob to arrange a marriage, but went off and married a Canaanite woman who bore him three sons in three years. Years passed, but Judah stayed away from the large campsite.

When Er, Judah's firstborn, reached maturity, Judah negotiated a marriage for him with a local young woman named Tamar. Judah hoped that marriage would have a civilizing effect on his wild son, but not even a new bride could leash his immoral practices, of which Judah only heard whispers. Er did not believe in Judah's God but in the Canaanite cults of his mother. One day the unimaginable happened, as Tamar came rushing in to her father-in-law:

"I can't wake him! He does not move! He is making strange sounds in his throat."

Judah hurried into Er's quarters in time to watch his firstborn die.

After the days of mourning passed, Judah called for his second son, Onan, and his daughter-in-law, Tamar. Addressing her first, he stated:

"You are childless, widow of my firstborn. The custom is for a childless widow to marry her dead husband's brother. The child born of such a union is the spiritual heir of the dead man and bears his lineage. This protects you, Tamar, for it keeps you within our household where you belong."

"Onan, you are to marry Tamar and do your duty. You have no choice just as she has no choice. I have spoken," and Judah waved them both away, giving orders to his wife to prepare for a minor feast for the next night.

Onan looked at Tamar lasciviously.

"You won't hear me complain about this. I've always been jealous of Er because of you," he said.

Tamar sighed to herself, but if this was her destiny, what could she do. Too bad none of Judah's sons was like Judah. He was so admirable, so powerful, so smart. They were smarmy puny creatures with no self-control and no intelligence. She was fascinated with Judah's stories of his family and his God, and wondered again why he did not live with them.

Tamar and Onan were married the next night. After being led into the bridal chamber, Onan almost attacked her in his impatience.

"Remember," she said, "your father said to remember that the levirate union is for Er, not for you."

Onan gritted his teeth and said, "No, I hated Er. I will not provide a son for his name's sake." Onan forced himself off of the mat, tried to stand up, made a strangled sound, and fell down on top of Tamar. When he did not move for over a minute, an almost crushed Tamar began yelling for help. Judah and his wife came rushing in with oil lamps in their hands, and beheld the insane scene. Judah bent down over Onan turning him on his back, thus freeing Tamar.

"He's dead. He is also dead," moaned Judah.

After the mourning period for his second son was over, Judah called for Tamar, but this time Shelah, his third son, was not called for.

"Tamar. I have decided to send you back to your father's house. Temporarily, of course. Yes, I know it's not done usually, but Shelah is still young and not ready to perform a levirate marriage. Remain a widow until I call for you." Judah would not meet her eyes, for her knew that his action was unacceptable, but he suspected that it was she who was responsible for the deaths of his two sons and feared for the life of his youngest. Everyone knew of these killer-widows; stories about them were told around many a campfire.

Powerless Tamar had no say, and she shamefully collected her few personal possession, and returned to her father's home. She wore widow's clothing that normally would announce to the world a widow's availability for remarriage, but she was not available. She was not free but chained to Judah's family because of the unbreakable custom of levirate marriage.

In her father's home, Tamar resumed the work she had done before her marriage. Her parents were ashamed of her, and she felt unwanted. She heard news from time to time of Judah's family, and calculated by the harvests that Shelah must have reached maturity. He was only a few years younger than Er. But she was not sent for and custom forbade her from approaching a patriarch.

News arrived the Judah's wife died. Tamar was indifferent to this news because even the short time that she spent with her had showed her that she was the one responsible for the corrupted sons. Again she waited. News came to town that Judah was off to northern pastures to shear the sheep, having completed his mourning for his wife.

"This is it," she said to herself. "Judah will never send for me. He fears that I am a killer-widow. If I do not do something myself, I will remain a childless widow forever in my father's house. If I can't have Shelah, then I will try to seduce Judah, for I must have a child. If he is going to the northern pastures, then he must pass the crossroads leading to Timna."

Tamar silently went into the room that she shared with her sisters, and found her beautiful veil, the one she had worn after her betrothal and up to her marriage. She wrapped it in a kerchief, along with a small vial of Egyptian perfume. Looking around to make sure no one was watching, she slipped out of the house, out of the town, towards the crossroads, which was some distance away. There was the marker and there was the god of the traveller in its usual niche. She stripped off her widow's clothing and carefully wrapped the long veil around her face and her body, anointing herself with the powerful jasmine scent.

"There he is in the distance. I would recognize his stride anywhere. And he's alone. What luck," she thought. She sat on the stone below the traveler's god, and assumed a seductive pose.

Judah noticed her and gradually slowed his pace. Looking at the idol and at her, he realized that she must be a temple prostitute, for only they and betrothed women wore veils. This was no betrothed woman.

Powerless Women: Dina and Tamar

But he did not recognize his daughter-in-law because of the veil and because it would never dawn on him that she could behave this way. Judah, knowing it was morally wrong, but unable to control himself, approached her.

"How much do you charge for your services?" he asked gruffly.

Her muffled voice replied, "What are you offering?"

"I have no payment with me but I will send a young goat from my flock as soon as I get there."

"You're asking me to trust you? I don't trust anyone. What can you give me as surety for your payment promise?"

"Whatever you suggest."

"I want your personal seal," she said pointing to the object dangling from his waist, "the cord to which it is attached," and eying Judah thoughtfully, "and your staff."

He handed the three objects to her and followed her into the small copse of trees. "Please, lord of Judah, give me fertility this time," thought Tamar. "I am not a bad woman, only a desperate powerless one with no other way out of an ugly situation."

As soon as Judah left, Tamar quickly stripped off the veil, folding it neatly again. She had her widow's robe on again and slowly made her way back to her father's home, hoping against hope for a change in her boring unproductive life.

Meanwhile Judah arrived at the shearing area and chose a young kid, sending it with his trusted friend Hira, for he did not want it known that he had been with a temple prostitute. He wanted his surety back and he was a man of his word. The woman could not eat his seal nor his staff. But Hira returned with the kid.

"I couldn't find her," he informed Judah. "And the local men said there never has been a temple prostitute at that crossroads."

"Let's drop the issue then. I certainly don't want to draw any attention to my actions. Let her keep the surety."

Three months later the whole town was buzzing. Tamar was pregnant. She would not talk about it. No one could figure out who the father was, although sharp tongues named a number of possibilities. What would Judah do? She was legally in his power. Was it considered adultery? She was a widow. But she was bound to a levirate marriage. But Judah had sent her away—didn't that free her?

Judah was informed of Tamar's pregnancy. To him this was adultery, and a solution to a problem which he had been putting off for some time. "Let her be taken out and burned as an adulterer!" As a patriarch he had the power of life and death over the members of his household.

"No trial? No questioning? No facing me?" shouted Tamar. "Just like that he said to execute me?" She pulled her younger brother into her room. "I have until sunrise. Please, please, I beg you. Take these three objects to my father-in-law and say exactly what I tell you to day. Swear that you will!"

The young man rushed off to Judah's encampment. He was greeted coldly but politely by the patriarch. Whipping out the staff, seal and cord from under his robe, the man stated: "By the man to whom these belong have I become pregnant, says Tamar."

Judah was stunned. His face flushed and he declared, "She is more just than I." He raced into town, gathered the elders together and declared publicly: "Tamar, my daughter-in-law, may have acted incorrectly, but so did I. It was my inaction that provoked her desperate action. It was my obligation to marry her to Shelah and I did not. I also sent her back to her father's house instead of keeping her with me, as I did not want to be reminded of my duty. She may have seduced me but I was also a willing participant. Let her go."

He faced Tamar who had been brought to the town's gates where all public events including trials took place.

"Come. Let's go home."

On the long walk back, Judah told Tamar that because of these events he realized that he could make major errors. How could he then blame his father for his errors? No one was perfect. Perhaps his sons had been so immoral because they had not been brought up in Jacob's household, but here, surrounded by Canaanite paganism. He had made a major decision: it was time to really go home.

Tamar, as the only wife of sorts in Judah's household, was responsible for overseeing the women's worlds until they joined Jacob's larger household. Then she became part of Leah's matriarchy. What a busy noisy place this was. Tamar felt at home at once, although she knew that her story had been told to all.

The midwife was called when the pain started in earnest. Leah helped her onto the birthstool, and said: "My first great-grandchild who is also my grandchild. What a strange situation."

"My lady," said the midwife who was kneeling in front of a laboring Tamar. "I will tie the red thread of the firstborn on this one. But the hand is drawn back inside, and the second is pushing out! A boy. And another boy. Double blessings, Tamar. Well done!"

Tamar, the labor over, was lowered from the birthstool onto the mat and covered with a colorfully woven thin rug. Leah washed her face and patted her head happily. With the two babies cleaned and swaddled, one on each side of her, Tamar was ready for Judah.

"Well," he said, looking from one to the other. "It's not quite a proper levirate, but this one," pointing to the baby with the scarlet band around his wrist, "will be name Zerah and is my grandson of Er. While this one will be named Peretz because he burst out first. He is my son." Judah looked at Peretz and said, "he really looks like some of my brothers."

"Judah," said Leah, he is the image of you!"

"Really," said Tamar. "I have a very good feeling about him." She drifted off to a half-sleep.

"You know that she is now free to marry whom she wishes," said Leah.

"I know," replied Judah. "Perhaps one of my nephews. I don't want to lose her. No, don't get me wrong—I would never cohabit with her again. I just feel a strong bond to her and want her to remain part of our larger family. After all, she is mother of my son. And my grandson."

"I won't leave you," whispered a half-awake Tamar. "Ever."

Jacob came to see the new additions and oversaw their circumcisions on the eighth day after their birth. Some of his sadness lifted, but his thoughts always drifted eventually to Joseph. He could not know that soon they would all be reunited in Egypt, nor that after happily settling there in Goshen, that a new pharaoh would enslave all of his descendants.

Notes

The Biblical texts for this chapter are Genesis 34 and 38.

For background material I recommend William Stiebling, *Ancient Near Eastern History and Culture* (Routledge, 2016); James Pritchard, ed., *The Ancient Near East* (Princeton University Press, 1958), Philip J. King and Lawrence Stager, *Life in Biblical Israel* (Westminster John Knox Press, 2001); Victor H. Matthews and Don C. Benjamin, *Social World of Ancient Israel, 1250-587 BCE* (Baker Academic, 2005); Jennie R. Ebeling, *Women's Lives in Biblical Times* (T & T Clark International, 2010), especially chapters 4 and 7.

Miriam and Tzippora: Sisters-in-Law

"I can't believe that mother had another baby, at such a dangerous time," thought Miriam as she walked through the tall bulrushes along the Nile River. "The Pharaoh gave the order to kill all Hebrew boy babies. As if that would weaken us anymore." She kept her eyes on the basket floating gently along the edge of the river, ignoring the stinging insects and interesting birds as she sidled along the reeds that just reached above her head. "But mother said that our God will protect us and our new baby. Some protection, with him floating in there with the hippopotami and crocodiles and snakes, and…" The basket turned with the current, and Miriam quickened her pace.

It seemed to her that she had been walking for hours since her mother had placed the water-proofed basket in the water near the slaves' quarters. Her father had left at sunrise along with all the other men to bake the bricks and work the quarries of Pharaoh's great building projects.

A bright colored bird flew right in front of Miriam's face, causing her to temporarily lose her concentration. She also watched an ibis catch a frog and after flipping it in the air, swallow it in one gulp. "Where is it?" she panicked and then calmed down as she caught sight of the basket heading towards the bathing enclosure right ahead. "It's going to get caught." She was about to step out of the reeds to free the basket when she heard voices.

"Come, your majesty. It's a beautiful day. You can swim here in safety and privacy," said a high-pitched voice.

"Enough, enough. I'll bathe when I want and I'll eat when I want and I wish you would all stop talking so much," said a deeper voice with an educated accent. "I just don't feel very happy right now."

"Oh your majesty, you'll get with child next month," said the young voice again.

"Stupid child, leave the princess alone. Don't you know how much it grieves her to be childless after all these years."

"The princess," thought Miriam, tiptoeing forward, with one eye on the basket. "I'm dying to see what Pharaoh's daughter looks like." She was at the very edge of the bulrushes but as her robe was the same beige color, as was her kerchief, Miriam blended in well. Now she could clearly see the stone walkway, and the stone steps leading into the water. Some slave women were setting up a divan and a small table with a bowl of fruit, and others were waving away the insects with long colorful feathers. One slave dressed all in white held an awning over a gorgeously dressed thin woman. Miriam could not see her features clearly, for her jeweled collar and bracelets almost blinded her.

The young slave who had been talking too much was poking around near the edge of the water. The princess glanced in her direction with an annoyed look on her face when she spied the basket caught in the net barrier just beyond.

"Look," she said. "Behind you. A basket. Fetch it for me and let's see what's in it. Let me open it."

"Yes, your majesty," said the slave as she gladly waded into the swimming area, enjoying the feel of the water as she went deeper. "I got it. I'll float it through here and push it toward you."

Miriam's heart almost stopped beating. "What is going to happen?" She watched the princess bend over and with great anticipation undo the clasp. "Please don't scream," prayed Miriam, "just coo your delicious baby sounds."

The baby cried softly as the lid was lifted and the sun hit his face.

"A baby," gasped the princess. "A Hebrew baby. For me."

"But princess, how do you know he's a Hebrew? And if he is, what could you possibly say to your father who has ordered them all to die?" asked the older slave.

"Of course he's a Hebrew. What woman except a totally desperate one would put a baby in a basket onto the dangerous waters of the Nile." Answered the princess. "As for my father, he'll say nothing, for this boy is a gift to me from the god of the Nile, a god more powerful than a pharaoh." She dandled the baby who continued to cry softly.

"He's hungry."

"Of course he's hungry."

"Where am I going to find a wetnurse? I need one now."

Miriam stepped forward out of the reeds, addressing the startled princess with all the seriousness of her seven years. "May I go and fetch a wetnurse from the Hebrews to nurse your child?"

The princess smiled at the serious girl, and said, "Yes, go and fetch one for my child. Quickly."

Miriam flew to the Hebrew section of the city and called her mother to come at once. Presenting her to the princess who was still bouncing the baby and walking up and down the stone walkway, refusing to allow her slaves to touch him, the princess said: "Take the child and nurse him for me. I will pay you and feed you well for his sake. Bring him to me in between the feedings so that I may play with him and love him. I have just named him Moses, because I drew him from the sacred water of the Nile."

Miriam was so happy that her baby brother was safe. The princess was so kind and so wise and Miriam watched Moses grow into a fearless four-year-old. But then he was weaned and moved permanently into the palace. For years Miriam saw so little of him that she barely recognized the adult Moses who came out to the building projects. She knew that he knew that his wetnurse was his real mother. She also knew that he was a firm believer in God. But why was his destiny connected to the palace, whereas she and all the other Hebrews labored in slavery? Even her marriage to Caleb ben Yefuneh and the birth of her first born were not entirely happy events because of the drudgery of the hard work. At least the newborn boys' lives were no longer in danger.

Miriam learned second-hand of the events that caused her brother to flee Egypt for Midian. Some of the story she heard from her fellow slaves, some of it from Moses, and some from his wife, Tzippora. Tzippora told her how Moses had appeared out of nowhere at the main oasis well. Unlike towns with their wells and civilized use of water, and, of course, unlike the villages along rivers like the Nile where you could use as much water as you wanted, semi-nomads only had the use of the wells at oases or at tribal centers. These wells were deep, often covered with large rocks, and it required much labor to lift the water to fill the troughs for the animals.

Tzippora and her six sisters used to have to wait their turn to use the well, as many of the shepherds arrived at the same time and the men pushed their way to the front of the line. That day she and her sisters had arrived early and filled the troughs, only to be pushed aside by the men before the animals had a chance to drink. It was at that point that Moses, who had been observing the scene unseen by anyone, jumped into the fray on the side of the women. He had beaten off the shepherds who were cowed by his fighting abilities and his bravery.

"He was wonderful!" Tzippora sighed. "How he hit them with his staff, his eyes burning with justice." Her own eyes glowed at the memory.

"We thanked him profusely and went to our father's tent area with the refreshed animals." Giggling and looking very young, Tzippora then imitated her father's deep voice.

"And how is it that you have returned so early today?" I said that an Egyptian man had saved us from the nasty Midianite men who wanted to steal our water." She turned to Miriam, adding as an aside. "I knew he was Egyptian because of his clothing and his funny accent. He would say "gamal" instead of "jamal," for instance." Returning to her story, Tzippora again deepened her voice imitating her father.

"A man saved you. A man alone. Probably a single man. And I have seven of you… Go fetch him and invite him to eat with us. Now!" We all fought over who would get to go and invite him. I won because I'm the oldest, but of course I took a couple of minutes to put on a more colorful headdress and to neaten up. Moses was still near the well trying to decide what to do. His face lit up when he saw me rushing back. I was so excited that I couldn't catch my breath. I felt so stupid just blurting out: "my father invites you to eat with us.'" She blushed under her suntan at the uncomfortable memory.

"I turned abruptly so that Moses would not see how embarrassed I was and marched to our tent. Moses rushed to keep up with me, saying, "Slow down. I've walked many lengths today. Is it your custom for women to be so free?" That stopped me in my tracks. "Free?" I asked him. "Free to work with the flocks, free to milk them, free to make cheese from the milk, leather from the skins, wool from the fleece, cloth from the wool. Then to come back to the tent and wait on our father and all his male guests? If so, then I'm free." He stood there seriously considering my outburst. "You are free because there is no one but your patriarch to tell you what to do and no one tells him what to do. You are free because you can wander where you will with your flocks under the open sky. You are free because you have no taskmaster to whip you." Looking into my eyes, he added, "You are free to turn down any man who does not please you."

"When you put it that way then I guess that I am free. But our life is harsh because the desert is harsh and we depend on the rain and the oasis and the desert plants."

"As we continued walking, now more slowly, Moses asked me, "What pleases you more than anything else?'" I was not used to such personal talk with a stranger and we were almost at our tent.

"Riding the half-wild horses of Arabia. Riding like the wind,' I responded, knowing that my passionate secret was safe with him. Moses smiled almost wistfully. "My riding is limited to horses trained in battle and parade. Maybe you could teach me to ride like the wind..." We reached the tent opening and he suddenly said, "You haven't told me your name."

"Tzippora," I whispered, "Tzippora, daughter of Yitro, priest of Midian, father of seven unmarried daughters."

"Welcome," boomed my father's voice. "Welcome to my humble tent, son of Egypt."

"My father really liked Moses. The bond between them grew over the next few weeks, as Moses offered to take on the job of shepherd, working alongside us so that he could learn how to find pasture, how to protect the sheep, and how to help the injured animals. Eventually he took this task on totally and we women could then focus our energies on the tasks of our tents. I missed the long walks in the silence and harsh beauty, and every so often I would join Moses for a day, always with another sister, of course. Our lifestyle never allows for unmarried women to be alone with any unrelated man.

"My father also grew closer to Moses as a result of their long talks. They discussed and compared their beliefs and Moses related the stories of the patriarchs and matriarchs, his monotheistic belief in God, and once in a while, he spoke of himself.

"I listened to these talks as I served them supper and drinks, and I added my own guesses to his sparse comments about himself. By that time we knew that he had been raised as a prince.

"My father taught him to write our language, and Moses responded by teaching him—and me, when no strangers were around—the Egyptian writing. It was so difficult because it was full of pictures. Our alphabet made much more sense because it followed the sounds that your mouth makes.

"And I would dream of him as I worked at grinding the grain, or baking the flatbreads, or spinning the wool, or cooking the meat. He was so handsome, so…so royal.

"One evening after supper, my father cleared his throat, and in an unusually formal voice said to Moses: "My son—if I may address you that way?" At Moses' smiling nod, my father continued. "I truly want you to be my son. I know that we are not wealthy nor do we live in stately palaces, but we are free and proud, and I would consider it an honor if you would become my son-in-law."

"My breath stopped in my throat. Moses also cleared his throat and replied: "It is I who am poor, for I have no brideswealth worthy of a man as proud as you."

"Brideswealth! You yourself said that your ancestor Jacob labored for seven years in exchange for brideswealth. You have guarded my flocks for over four months now, and I am willing—by becoming your patriarch for you will live here within my tents—to accept your labor as brideswealth too. My clan knows of you and values you, so there will be no shame in this exchange."

"I was still holding my breath, for my father had not said which daughter, and all of my sisters wanted Moses. As a matter of fact, the squabbling among us was almost unbearable.

"Moses then replied: "If it is acceptable to you, then it also is to me. And you must forgive me for having to negotiate my own marriage terms, as there is no one to talk for me."

"Of course, of course," my father said, waving this aside with a brief hand gesture.

They sat silently, smiling at each other, when Moses suddenly asked, "But which daughter? You have seven."

"By now we were all listening in, poking our heads through all the ten flaps, elbowing each other.

"Yes, I have seven daughters, each one more charming than the next, each well educated indeed." I knew that he was referring to me, as none of my sisters could read or write very well.

"You choose, Moses. That way I will not be heaped with blame." We all silently groaned, and elbowed up even closer.

"You do not have the custom of marrying the oldest first?" Moses asked.

"No. Why should we? We marry off our daughters to the men we consider suitable for them—and for us, of course."

"How wise," Moses replied. "I shuddered thinking that as the oldest I had just gone down a peg. But Moses then said forcefully, "I choose Tzippora."

"Hooray!" I shouted out loud, quickly covering my mouth and scurrying out of the public tent area so that my father would not catch me there. My sisters withdrew as well, some crying in frustration. But after a few minutes they all gathered around to congratulate me.

"Then came the wedding preparations. We desert dwellers do not have a long betrothal period, in part because we marry when all the clans are gathered at the specific times of the year when we meet to confer on clan matters. We have judgements then, we sell our wool and cloth then, and we have our weddings then. When my father and Moses agreed on the marriage, it was at the time of the clan gathering.

"Over the years, each of my sisters and I had set aside time to work on our personal special clothing. Our embroidery is famous for its bold reds of many hues. I had also bought—from the silver that was mine from selling the cheese of my personal sheep—a beautiful pair of sandals, totally luxurious because they were too delicate to wear outside of the tent.

"My sisters helped me with my bath and Moses had given me some Egyptian perfume in the tiniest glass vial I had ever seen. One of my sisters braided my hair into dozens of thin plaits, piling one on the other into a kind of black crown. I refused to color my hair with henna knowing that Moses really admired my raven-colored tresses. Then, when I was almost ready, my father came into the tent and presented me with a set of silver jewelry, for my ears, my brow, my arms, my wrists, my ankles and my neck. He did something that he had not done since I was twelve—he bent down and kissed my cheeks.

"Tzippora, you look like a queen of the desert, with your black hair and eyes, your sun-darkened skin, and your glow of happiness. May your marriage to Moses be fruitful and happy. I know that you love him already." Then he added something strangely prophetic. "Beware not to love him too much." But I was too elated to pay attention to his warning.

"I was led from the women's tent into the public area to the sounds of drums, tabors, flutes and song. It was enough for me to see Moses" face light up to cancel any doubts that I still had about his secret past and perhaps even an unforgettable Egyptian love. I danced the bride's dance before him whirling faster and faster to the drumbeat, until the heart stopping halt of all sound, when I sank to my knees, head down on my extended arms. Moses arose and bent down to take both of my hands in his, lifting me up, to the applause and cheers of the wedding guests. Then we rushed out to our own private new tent."

"Yes," said Tzipporah, "life was sweet and simple then. We had the two boys, and Moses watched the flocks. Little did I know that God would choose him to lead the Israelites out of Egypt. He told you about his first confrontation with God via the burning bush, right? Life was never the same after that day. When he returned from the desert his face had changed, and he went immediately to my father to get permission to return to Egypt, and permission for me and the boys to leave. After all, it meant a total change in our marriage contract."

"So you left together. But had you not just given birth?"

"Yes. That was the problem. Eliezer had not been circumcised yet, and Moses put it off knowing we would be traveling through the desert.

At the caravanserai, that night, the Angel of Death almost killed Moses for not fulfilling this most basic commandment."

"What did you do?"

"I am a daughter of the desert, which means I am very practical and swift. I grabbed the flintstone and circumcised the baby. I had seen it done many times, for we Midianites also circumcise our males, as do Arabs. As soon as I had done so, Moses was fine."

"So what happened?"

"I made the worst mistake of my life then," sighed Tzippora. "I agreed to return to my father's home with the boys until Eliezer would recuperate and my husband would call for me. He never sent for me. It's as though he forgot we existed. If not for my father's insistence to come to Moses, my being sent home could have served legally as a divorce."

"Yes, while you turned back, we underwent the most exciting and inconceivable experiences ever. God sent ten plagues, then we fled to the Sea of Reeds, where we fearfully watched the approaching Egyptian army. We thought we were doomed but then the sea split and we rushed across. God spoke to me then, Tzipporah, and I led the women in the mass celebration of triumph. What a glorious time we had, dancing with the drums and the tambourines, swirling round and round."

"I heard, Miriam. I am sorry I missed it all."

"You did not miss everything, for we are all now headed for Mount Sinai to receive God's laws, and then we are all going to the land that God promised our ancestors."

Miriam looked at her beautiful dark sister-in-law in sympathy. She knew that once Moses had experienced God, he had stopped living with his wife. Despite the fact that both she and Aaron had also experienced prophecy, they still lived with their spouses.

"Let me talk to Aaron and we will both talk to Moses for your sake, Tzippora." Miriam patted Tzippora's hand, her mind planning out how to approach her unapproachable younger brother. She would not be treated as "just a woman." Moses should know better, that Israelite women were strong and had specific rights both by law and by custom. But poor Tzippora. She so loved her husband.

Miriam remembered Yitro's arrival in the Israelite camp, a proud thin man with a hawklike face, riding in on a beautiful Arabian horse, with a small boy holding on to his waist followed by his attractive daughter, on a smaller horse with a baby strapped over her body in an intricate series of ties that both supported the child and gave the mother freedom to use her hands.

The two horses rode into the midst of the thousands of people who were camped in their tribal units. It was unbelievable how well organized the entire army of people was. Yitro was directed to the very center where, and only when he saw Moses, did he dismount.

"Father-in-law! Welcome!" Greeted Moses.

"I am glad to hear you address me as such," declared Yitro for all to hear. "Here is your wife and your two sons who you seem to have forgotten to send for." Moses greeted them, and Gershom shyly came to take his father's hand. Shown the way to his tent, Tzippora disappeared into the private rear section where she quickly took over the wifely duties expected of her. Her father meanwhile sat in the front public part, listening to the stories of Moses' escapades, his hair standing on end as Moses talked. Tzippora could hear everything as she prepared mint tea for the men, and began supper for what appeared to be a horde of men who kept coming to meet her father. But the wives of the men came into the work part of the tent with roasted meats, flat breads, fruit, and water. This sharing seemed to be something very Israelite.

Tzippora shyly greeted each of the women, who were curious to see Moses' wife. Her brightly colored clothing and jangling silver bracelets and earrings were new to them, as was her suntanned skin. Midianite women were dark to start with, having come from Cush or Ethiopia. Staying out in the sun made them even darker, unlike Egyptian women who avoided the sun's rays like the plague.

Tzippora finally met Miriam, of whom Moses had talked quite a bit. They took an instant liking to each other, and Miriam admired the proud carriage of her sister-in-law. She had already heard about her feats of horsemanship. "We certainly grew up in different world," stated Miriam. "You grew up as free as the wind, whereas I... well that chapter is over now. Now I too am free, but it does take some getting used to."

Miriam and Tzippora: Sisters-in-Law

The opportunity to speak to Moses privately did not present itself for some time, as Moses was busy with the construction of the portable Sanctuary with its outer court, inner court, and Holy of Holies. There was a need not only for wood for the structure but for fabrics for curtains and precious metals for the altars and implements and vessels to be used in the rituals. Everyone in the vast camp was inspired to contribute to the construction of the Sanctuary, and the women donated not only their jewelry made of precious metals but also their skills at spinning and weaving.

Miriam surveyed all the activity and listened to the excitement in the women's sections, as they sat many long hours spinning and weaving. What made the time pass more quickly was the group aspect of these activities, for she saw extended families of women, sometimes four generations, performing this pious act of love. She overheard young women wondering aloud where their pieces of fabric would hang. Blue, purple, white, and scarlet linen cloth was folded and collected. The finest was set aside for Aaron's garments, for he had become the Kohen Gadol, or High Priest; his four sons were to assist him.

Momentarily a feeling of envy passed through Miriam as she saw the political and religious leadership roles of her two brothers, but in acknowledging the respectful greetings of all the Israelite women as she passed, she recognized that her position was important as well.

Finally the Sanctuary was ready. The artists—Bezalel and Aholiyav—had performed a miracle, for the time had been short and the task arduous, but the workers who were fired with religious enthusiasm completed the work. The Sanctuary and the Tabernacle were raised and the offerings were presented, and Miriam and the women participated in the joy and celebration. She knew that this marked a major break from other religions, in that women were to have access to the Sanctuary. There would be no fertility priestesses nor any immoral activities connected with God's house. The Sanctuary would wean the Israelites from idolatry and turn them to God. The detailed rituals would mold them into a spiritual people for it was visible proof to the people that God was among them.

Finally, after the inauguration of the Sanctuary service and the consecration of Aaron and his sons, Miriam felt that she could wait no longer. The sight of her sad faced sister-in-law pushed her to approach Aaron, who also sympathized with Tzippora's plight. Miriam, comfortable in her relationship with Aaron, said to him privately: "What shall we do? Why should Moses not live with Tzippora?" Aaron's nodding encouraged Miriam to continue. "Did not God speak to us as well, and yet we remain living with our spouses."

Suddenly God's voice filled their ears, summoning them to the Tabernacle. Miriam and Aaron quickly if fearfully obeyed, meeting Moses in the holy structure. The pillar of cloud, declaring God's presence, lowered to envelope the tent. God's voice then summoned Miriam and Aaron forward. The voice was like no other voice and Miriam was not sure if it came from within or without her head. Glancing at Aaron she realized that he was experiencing the same thing. The voice explained that all other prophets experienced prophecy as a vision or a dream, except for Moses. God's relationship with Moses was so unique it was almost face to face. Therefore why did the two of you speak against God's modest servant?

The divine anger was palpable as the cloud lifted. Aaron turned to her to share his experience but when he saw Miriam he gasped. She had become a leper. Her skin had taken on the splotchy coloration so characteristic of the disease, and her nose and ears looked almost black.

"What? What?" she asked in fear at her brother's expression. But Aaron turned from her to Moses who had seen the entire thing. "Please, Moses, please. We may have acted foolishly and we may have sinned. But please, do not let our sister be as a dead person with her flesh half consumed!"

Miriam stood in shock realizing that Aaron's references meant that she had been punished with leprosy, the traditional punishment for speaking ill of others. Briefly the thought flitted across her mind: "Why only me? Why not Aaron as well? Just as briefly she replied to herself: "Perhaps because it would destroy his ritual purity, and he must lead the worship of God."

As from a distance she watched her two brothers, the older begging the younger, the younger looking straight at her, compassion written all over his face. Moses then shouted from the depths of his heart: "Please God, heal her now!"

The two brothers seemed to hold their collective breath. As their faces changed from compassion and concern to relief, Miriam braved a glance at her hands. The telltale leprous colors were gone. With tears flowing, she humbly accepted God's dictum that she be shut away for a week, as symbol of the shame of public punishment by God acting as a spiritual parent and teaching a child a serious lesson in proper behavior. During the week of public shame the entire camp of Israelites waited for her. She had time to contemplate her actions and her life. She continued to feel compassion for Tzippora, but there was nothing she could do. Moses not only was separated from her, but from their sons as well. Again the Israelites were moving away from the norm of Middle Eastern behavior. There was no guarantee that a son, let alone a first-born son, would inherit the mantle of leadership from a powerful father. Talent counted, as did the teacher-disciple relationship, as well as the active interference of God.

Miriam lived out the rest of her life in the Sinai desert, disappointed that she would not be entering the land of Israel, but content—unlike Aaron and Moses—that her husband as well as her children would take part in the conquest.

Notes

The Biblical texts for this chapter are Exodus 1-5, 15:20-21, 18:1-12, and Numbers 12.

For background material, I recommend Barbara Watterson, *Women in Ancient Egypt* (Stroud, 2013); Lise Mannich, *Sacred Luxuries: Fragrance, Aromatherapy, and Cosmetics in Ancient Egypt* (Cornell University Press, 1999); Israel Eph'al, *The Ancient Arabs: Nomads on the Borders of the Fertile Crescent, 9-5 Centuries BC* (Magnes Press, 1982); Gershon Galil, *The Ancient Near East in the 12th–10th Centuries BCE: Culture and History: Proceedings of the International Conference held at the University of Haifa, 2-5 May 2010* (Ugarit-Verlag, 2012); E. W. Barber, *Women's Work: the First 20,000 Years. Women, Cloth, and Society in Early Times* (W. W. Norton, 1994); Jennie R. Ebeling, *Women's Lives in Biblical Times* (T & T Clark International, 2010), especially chapters 2 and 4.

Deborah the Judge

"What is going on?" the farmer asked his neighbor in the town of Ramah. He watched people hurry past his small home heading for the hill country in the distance. "Did something happen in Beit-el?"

"Where have you been?" responded the older man, stopping in the midst of putting a thick blanket on his donkey. "Haven't you heard the news? We have a new Judge. Everyone is going to meet God's newly appointed leader." Turning back to his donkey, he finished preparing it for his ride.

"God sent a leader to unite us against our enemies. Halleluya! Wait for me. I want to see him too."

The old man turned back and with a wicked grin said, "Him? Who said the Judge is a him? Her name is Deborah." With that he kicked his donkey, leaving the neighbor with his jaw dropped in astonishment, the same astonishment each man had initially felt upon hearing the news. Like the others, the farmer thought further. "Why not?" he said to himself. "It's the Lord's choice. The Lord can choose a farmer, a shepherd, an illegitimate, or a warrior. What the Lord chooses is up to the Lord. It is our job to follow. So why not a woman?" With that, he rushed into his modest house calling to his tired wife. "Come, let's go up to the hills to see Deborah the Judge."

The people came from all over the tribal portion of Ephraim to Deborah for judgement. She sat outdoors, in the shade of an old palm tree and patiently heard the quarrels of neighbors, of strangers, of brothers, of co-wives. They all waited their turns, giving space to the complainers to present their cases in relative privacy. Now and then those on line could hear snatches of words, but never precisely what was going on. As each group was given her judgement, there were few complaints, for the people knew that she was divinely inspired.

The line moved slowly forward. The assistants gave the signal for the next group to stand in judgement. The first impression that the people had of her was her gray-blue eyes which seemed to pierce to their very souls. One could not lie nor exaggerate to eyes like that. Her slender hawklike nose added to the impression of aristocracy and authority. Her mouth neither smiled nor frowned but was set in a neutral line. It was only when she spoke that her warmth shone forth, for her voice was deep and vibrant, and her clear enunciation of her words made what she said almost musical.

After some time had passed and the people had become used to Deborah's manner and decision-making style, a group of elders decided that the time was right to approach her.

"What is it that bothers you, elders of the tribes of Issachar, Dan, Zevulun, Naphtali, Reuven, Ephraim, and Benjamin? Surely there is no legal matter so great as to cause so many respected patriarchs to gather together to talk to me."

The men hesitated, unsure of who should be the spokesman for the group. Finally, one powerfully built leader of the tribe of Zevulun stepped forward and in a deep basso voice, easily heard by all gathered there, said:

"Greetings, oh Deborah the Judge. We the leaders of the tribes of the hill country and the coast have come to you to state our puzzlement."

"Puzzlement, oh patriarch of Zevulun? Please elaborate."

"We know from past experience, that since the death of Joshua, disciple of Moshe, there has been no leader of all of the tribes of Israel. We have been conquering the land gradually, but have stayed within our tribal units. The only time that we have united is when God has chosen a leader, a Judge, to lead us against a specific enemy. Our enemy is Yavin the Canaanite king who, over the past many years, has almost enslaved us. He has imported weapons of iron from the kingdoms of the far north and has forbidden us from using any metal at all. Do you know how difficult it is to plow with only wood?" The other men nodded vigorously in assent. A second elder, older but with a voice just as vigorous, picked up the pace by taking over.

"Yavin has managed to control not just the metal production in our land, but also all of our main roads and highways. We must pay dearly to transport goods even on a local level. And how has he done this? Because he has a standing army of over 900 chariots!"

The others nodded again, and a third, younger elder, this time of Reuven, took over:

"These chariots are not just wheeled vehicles made out of wood and leather, but are lethal weapons in themselves. They are built with metal spokes protruding from the central wheel axis. In other words, a rider has to merely drive down a road and these protrusions will cut to ribbons anyone on foot, be he a simple farmer or an infantryman."

Deborah sat patiently through these ardent speeches. She nodded from time to time, encouraging the men to get to the point.

"So…" the speaker hesitated.

"So?" Deborah asked.

The first speaker jumped back in. "So when are you going to lead us against Yavin? What miracle will God perform to save us from this despot?"

"Ah!" breathed Deborah. She slowly rose from the stump of the palm tree on which she had been seated. Taller than the majority of the men already, and standing on a higher part of the hill, Deborah loomed above the group.

"First of all," she enunciated in her bell-like tone. "God chooses the time for action, not I. I merely obey orders." Then, slowly looking into the eyes of each man in turn, she added: "and you are relying on a miracle to get you out of this situation? You think you are of Moshe's generation? To be saved from Yavin, you yourselves may very well have to go to war! Are you prepared to do so?"

Some of the men met her icy-blue stare, but most averted their eyes almost at once.

"I see. Some of you are, but some are not. Let me not unduly influence you, as the Lord has not yet clearly communicated with me. When God does, you will all be informed immediately. Good evening, patriarchs all. I will now go home for the evening meal. Go in peace."

The Biblical Woman

With that, Deborah pulled her cloak around her, and, escorted by her disciples, began the trek back to her home where servants had the evening meal prepared according to the orders she had left with them early that morning.

At approximately the same time that Deborah was returning home, miles away in the city-state of Yavin the Canaanite king, two people came to a crucial decision. Hever, seated on the carpet next to the copper tray on its tripod, leaned over to take a flatbread and began tearing it apart. Using the pieces as a means of conveying the tangy cooked beans and chickpeas into his mouth, he said: "Stop hovering over me, Yael. Sit down and eat with me. We have no guests for you to serve." Yael looked around and said: "But the slaves will talk."

"Who cares what slaves say?" Hever continued to eat, taking sips of wine every now and then. "Sit near me and hear my decision. I will only do this, however, if you agree."

Yael lowered herself gracefully onto the carpet, helping herself to some fresh dates. She guessed what Hever was about to say, but waited patiently for him to say it. She had learned years ago, at the start of their marriage, that this was the best way to get along with her husband.

"You know how we Kenites have been closely allied with the Israelites ever since Moshe married one of our women?" At Yael's nod, Hever continued. "Well, I personally am very impressed both with their God and with their way of life. Everything they do is imbued with a sense of specialness, of closeness to their God. What do you say, Yael?"

"I agree, my husband, and if I may add, I like the way of life of their women. Why look at their leader—Deborah the Judge. They play much more important roles in all parts of life, unlike the Canaanite women who are practically the slaves of their fathers and husbands."

Heber flashed a smile at his wife.

"So what do you say about moving into the Israelite territory and joining them?"

"You mean cutting our ties with King Yavin?" asked Yael. "Will that not be dangerous?"

"It may be, but I have found an excellent camp site in the huge valley facing Mount Tabor. It is near enough to the Kishon river to make water easily available for our flock, yet far enough away to avoid any of the spring floods. Let's do it Yael, and get away from this sinful Canaanite city. We belong out in the open." Hever stopped eating and was looking earnestly at his wife.

Yael daintily put down the date pit and, facing her husband, said: "You have already become Israelite by asking my concurrence. Of course I agree. We can be packed up and on our way by late morning. It will be wonderful to be out in the open again. But," she added hesitantly, "I have a strange sensation about this move, as though something very dangerous is to occur."

"Nonsense," said Hever, picking up a bunch of grapes, "it's your overactive imagination."

While the Kenite couple slowly made their way in the direction of the Valley of Jezreel and Mount Tabor, Deborah the Judge had a divine vision. She immediately sent a messenger riding as fast as he could to the home of Barak, son of Avinoam, in the hill country of Naftali. Meanwhile Deborah went out, as had become her habit, to the hill where she sat in judgement. By late afternoon she saw the dust of horseriders rising in the distance. By nightfall a dusty and thirsty small group of men arrived. They were given food and shelter for the night in the richest home of Ramah, and in the morning Barak presented himself to Deborah. She looked at the fierce face of the man, standing like an immovable force in front of her, and nodded as if in agreement.

"Good morning Barak, son of Avinoam. I thank you for obeying my summons in a timely fashion."

"Peace be with you, Deborah the Judge, " Barak growled in his gritty voice. "It is not every day that I get a call to appear before God's representative."

"Yes," she replied. "This is the Lord's call to you. God has commanded you to gather an army of ten thousand men of the children of Naftali and Zevulun. With these men you are to march up to Mount Tabor. Then the Lord will draw near to you Sisera, captain of Yavin's military force with his chariots and army. Thus says the Lord: "I will deliver him into your hand!"

When Deborah delivered this message, her bell-like voice deepened into a gong-like sound, and her eyes were focused at mid-distance. When she finished, she looked directly at Barak, awaiting his response.

He thought for a moment before responding, much to Deborah's surprise. "If you will go with me then I will go; but if you will not go with me, then I will not go."

Deborah's thoughts moved in two directions simultaneously. Either he wants me to go because he feels that I will inspire the men with my presence. Or he wants me to go because he doesn't trust me—that way if the battle is lost, he and all Israel will blame me and not him!

Aloud Deborah said: "I will surely go with you. But Barak, son of Avinoam, remember, I gave you the opportunity to be a national hero, the center of all honor. My going will diminish that honor." Her voice deepened once more as she added prophetically: "The Lord will give Sisera over into the hand of a woman."

Regaining her normal voice and demeanor, Deborah ordered Barak to send out the call to all the tribes to send men to meet them at Kedesh where they would climb Mount Tabor. But only two tribes were brave enough to send men, namely Zevulun and Naftali. The others were too fearful, as Deborah had predicted.

Within three day, ten thousand foot soldiers from the two tribes, armed with whatever weapons they had hidden away from the Canaanites met Barak at Mount Tabor on the side facing the river Kishon. Deborah had travelled on her grey mule alongside Barak, exhilarated by the action and movement. Her eyes took in everything, but she did not discuss her thoughts with Barak who kept muttering to himself: "Why Mount Tabor? Why on the side of the river?" Yet since it was God's command, that is where Barak assembled the men.

They were all organized by Barak, a natural military leader, who divided them into groups, each headed by tribal and clan leaders. Camp was set up, and the men went about the ordinary tasks of setting up cooking areas, sleeping sections, and primitive latrines apart from the camp. Some men climbed down the slope to fetch water for their units, others sharpened their weapons. All awaited the upcoming battle with a combination of bravery and fear. Barak, camped on the slope above the men, but at a good distance from Deborah's small encampment, kept looking eastward for signs of an approaching army.

To the east, a rider had wildly entered the Canaanite city-state, rushing almost into the palace on his animal. The guard stopped him, but he jumped off his mule shouting: "My lord Sisera, my lord Sisera!" A soldier ran in to bring the man to the commander of the forces. Sisera was seated in a lavishly decorated room, next to an older woman, obviously his mother from the physical resemblance of the two.

"Speak," he said to the sweaty rider.

"My lord Sisera! I ride from the hill country of the Israelites. Barak, son of Avinoam, has gathered an army of ten thousand up on Mount Tabor. And that woman, that judge or whatever, has gone with Barak. It's a rebellion!"

Sisera arose with a big smile on his face. "A battle! Excellent. It will give me a chance to try out my new chariots-of-war on a real army."

To the officers in the room he began to give orders to gather the army of charioteers as well as the infantry. To his personal guard, Sisera gave orders to get his uniform and battle standard ready. To one officer he gave directions on loading up food for the soldiers, and to another he told to dispense the weapons from the storehouse. To his mother, Sisera said: "Farewell. I will return within the week victorious as always, with a special gift for you. Perhaps a new Israelite slave girl?"

Within hours the people of the city-state were cheering the army of chariots on its way, with King Yavin himself coming to the city gates to bless Sisera and all the men. "Return victorious!" They all shouted and waved. The wheels rumbled and the divisions of nine hundred chariots rolled westward toward Mount Tabor and their destiny.

The next morning, so early that one could barely make out shapes, Barak awakened to the voice of Deborah who was standing at the opening of his tent. "Up!" she ordered, "for this is the day in which the Lord will deliver Sisera into your hand!"

Barak leapt up and rushed outdoors. The day was not normal, and it took Barak a moment to realize what was different. The sun was rising brightly in the east, but there were ominous black clouds on the horizon to the west. "Rain?" he groaned. "Rain in the spring! How will that help us?" To the east he finally saw what he had been searching for, a huge dust cloud slowly nearing the mountain. "Sisera's army approaches, and the Lord sends us rain to make the fighting even more difficult!"

"Are you really a military man?" asked Deborah. "Don't you see that this will even our chances. They have the armor and the chariots, but the rain will swell the river, that river to which you could not understand why the Lord directed you. They will have to fight on foot, Barak, so that it will be up to our brave men, inspired by the Lord, to win in an otherwise equal fight!"

The light went on in Barak's eyes. "You're right, Deborah. How simple and how complex at the same time. Look at the rain clouds swelling towards us. And we have the advantage of attacking from above." Turning toward his men, he trumpeted his orders: "Up men, for today the Lord has delivered the Canaanite army into our hands!"

They all watched with bated breath as Sisera's chariots got into formation. The sun from the east was reflected on the armor and the metal sides of the chariots. But the rain clouds rolled in just then and with a huge burst of thunder and lightening, the clouds emptied their load of water which rushed down the mountainside to swell the almost dry river with an angry flood of grey water. Just then Sisera gave the order to charge. Ignoring the sudden cloudburst, the chariots moved forward, but as they reached the banks of the Kishon, the drivers hesitated. "On, on, it's a passing rain cloud! On, on!" Urged Sisera.

The charioteers whipped their horses on. The horses plunged into the water, but the river bed had become a muddy mess and the heavy wheels, spokes and all, became enmired. The drivers tried to move, but to no avail.

Meanwhile, Barak had the shofar blasts sounded for the charge of the Israelites. Down the hillside rushed the ten thousand men, shouting in the name of God, inspired by what they saw before them and by Deborah behind them. The Canaanites leaped off their chariots, but they were unused to fighting as infantry, and so, despite their weaponry advantage, the Israelites quickly gained the upper hand.

Sisera watched the fighting, quickly assessed his chances. Leaping out of his chariot in order to evade recognition—for his chariot markers showed his military rank—he threw off his cloak of rank and headed towards the open valley. The dust raised by the fighting completed his disguise, and he briefly, if regretfully, watched his empty chariot skewing this way and that as his horse bucked through the crowd.

A few hours later, Sisera found himself climbing up a gradually rising hill. Tired and unbelievably thirsty, he saw a large black tent about two hundred feet ahead. He stopped dead in his tracks until he noticed that the tribal markings on the tent were Kenite. "Kenites," he thought, "friends of Canaan."

As he approached the tent, a woman emerged from the tent who looked him over from the distance. She motioned for him to come closer, saying to Sisera, "Turn in, my lord, turn in here to me. Do not fear."

"Water," Sisera croaked. "Water, please."

"Sit, my lord. I will fetch you a drink. But my lord shivers. I will fetch a cover for my lord." As Sisera sat, Yael rushed to get him a light woolen blanket, thinking rapidly. "What do I do now? Surely it's Sisera. I recognize him from all those parades in King Yavin's city-state. He's the enemy of Israel. We are now becoming Israelites. Hever is actually fighting in Barak's army on Mount Tabor. Be brave, Yael. Think! Think!"

After covering him, Yael went to get some water for Sisera, but on the way she noticed the container of milk hanging from a peg near the water jug. "Milk, I'll give him milk to make him sleepy. That will give me time to think!"

She reached for the leather canteen and gave Sisera the fresh goat's milk to drink. He greedily swallowed almost the entire thing. Yael fixed the cover over him, noting that the shaking had ceased.

Sisera, in a tired voice, ordered Yael to stand guard at the tent opening. "Stand there and if any man asks you "Is there any one here?" you will say "no"." Yael nodded and went to the tent opening. From time to time she glanced back at Sisera who lay back, and in a few minutes was breathing heavily and evenly.

"Unbelievable", Yael thought. "He must have escaped the battle and here he is fast asleep. I don't have a sword because Hever is using it. I don't even have a large knife. I have no weapon, and Sisera is sleeping atop his own sword. What can I use?"

Her eyes swept over the tent's interior. Nothing useable. From the opening she looked at the outside of the tent and her eyes fell on the large wooden mallet thoughtlessly left lying next to the extra tent peg, left last night as they had rushed to erect the large tent before nightfall.

Her eyes returned to the mallet and the tent peg. An idea leapt into her mind. She looked at Sisera, and seeing that he was indeed fast asleep, she silently stepped outside toward the two objects. A slave rushed out just then to grab them out of the way, but Yael motioned her away. Bending down, she picked them up, and slowly moving back to the tent opening, she tested the sharpness of the peg on her hand. The blood that spurted from her palm convinced her that this was indeed a sharp object.

Slowly she moved step by step up to the sleeping man. "Now I must get it right the first time, or he will awake and kill me. I can't pierce his heart, and I'm not sure where to pierce his neck; I only know how to slice that. The head. I'll have to pierce his head at the softest spot. That means the temple."

Just then Sisera changed position, turning from his back onto his side. Yael stood over him, and with a prayer to the God of Israel, placed the sharp end of the peg next to Sisera's right temple and slammed the flat end with the mallet a hard as she could. The pin went right through his head and into the ground. He let out a sigh and died.

The sound of approaching footsteps aroused Yael out of her hypnotic state. She had no idea how long she had knelt there, frozen. She arose and went to the tent opening just as a large gruff man approached. Recognizing Barak from her husband's description, Yael said to him: "Come and I will show you the man whom you seek."

Pushing aside the tent flap, Barak followed her inside and beheld the dead Sisera, with the tent peg in his temples. Looking at her with wonder on his face, Barak asked her name.

"Blessed are you Yael, wife of Hever. Come with me to meet Deborah the Judge, and to be presented to our triumphant army as the slayer of Sisera."

Yael took her cloak, as Barak gave orders to his men to transport Sisera's dead body on a donkey. They all walked together in the direction of Mount Tabor, where the dead were already being buried and the living Canaanites were being counted and divided up into slave groups. The armor was being piled up, to be divided later, as were all the animals, and all the confiscated goods.

Yael walked on, next to Barak, and the Israelites stopped to watch. From the left she heard Hever's voice. "Yael, Yael, what are you doing here? What happened?" On the nod from Barak, he joined the group heading up the hillside to the woman who was overlooking all the events.

Deborah stepped forward to greet Yael. "It is you! You are the deliverer of the Israelites. You are the slayer of Sisera!" Yael nodded, speechless at meeting the blue eyes of Deborah. Deborah smiled and said: "Yael, you will live forever in the hearts of Israel." She grabbed a small drum, and with a look of great concentration, Deborah began to beat out a rhythm. The men all stopped what they were doing to listen. In a strong voice, accompanied by her drum, Deborah intoned a triumphal poem, half chanted, half sung, a poem of deliverance and praise. Her song described the oppression of Israel, the gathering of the tribes, the battle, and the defeat of the enemy. She castigated the tribes that were not brave enough to fight, and she praised those that did. Her voice rose and fell in poetic cadences. Looking at Yael, she intoned:

> Blessed above women shall Yael be,
> The wife of Hever the Kenite,
> Above tenting women shall she be blessed.
> Water he asked, milk she gave him
> In a royal bowl she gave him curd.
> Her hand she put to the tent peg
> Her right hand to the mallet;
> And with the mallet she smote Sisera,
> She smote him through his head.
> Yes, she pierced and struck through his temples.
> At her feet he sank, he fell, he lay;
> At her feet he sank, he fell;
> While he sank, there he fell down dead.

Yael almost cried with pride and joy. She had no thought of being heroic when she had killed Sisera; she had merely done what she thought was morally right.

All the Israelites gathered repeated the final words of Deborah's lyrical poem, soon to be memorized and recited throughout the land, and then to be recorded in the Book of Judges. "So may all your enemies perish, Oh Lord, but they that love God shall be as the sun which shines with all its' might."

Notes

The Biblical texts for this chapter are Judges 4:5. The translation of the poem is from the Tanakh of the Jewish Publication Society.

For background material, I recommend James M. Miller and John H. Hayes, *A History of Ancient Israel and Judah* (John Knox Press, 2006); F. W. Dobbs-Allsopp, *On Biblical Poetry* (Oxford University Press, 2015), chapters 3 and 4; Morris Silver, *Prophets and Markets: The Political Economy of Ancient Israel* (Kluwer Academic Publishing, 1982), chapters 5-10.

Ruth

"What do you mean, your mother will not attend the wedding?" the large hawk-eyed man growled at Mahlon. "Such things are not done in Moab."

"If you please, sire, my mother is an old-fashioned Israelite and the women seclude themselves in widowhood." Mahlon's heart was in his mouth, knowing what a lie he was saying. His mother in seclusion! His mother had just castigated him for arranging his own marriage, and worse yet, to a Moabite.

"You would think that after all these years of living in Moab she would change, but, alas, the older she gets the more she reverts to the old ways." Mahlon added.

"Yes, yes," grumbled his future father-in-law. "I well remember my Egyptian-born grandmother who in her old age refused to speak anything but Egyptian." Turning to his chief slave he ordered: "Let the music begin and have all the food and drinks served. Tonight I give my last daughter in marriage."

Nervous and excited, Mahlon retired to the room reserved for the groom and his anxiously awaiting brother Hilion.

"Well, what did he say?" Hilion whispered.

"He accepted the excuse. I will be married in an hour. You can now use the same excuse with Orpa's father, for I'm sure he too will accept mother's absence as a peccadillo of old age."

"Old age! Mother is barely forty and tough as nails."

"Yes, but they do not know that. They only know that we came to Moab from Bethlehem and have been living here for over a decade. For them that is time enough to become Moabite. They can't know that mother only talks of returning "home", while we consider Moab "home". They also can't know that we are acting improperly by arranging our own marriages."

Just then the slaves came to bring Mahlon into the main room for the marriage ceremony.

"Mother, please meet my new wife. Her name is Ruth."

Naomi stood stiffly at the window with her back to her son. Slowly she turned around prepared to hate her Moabite daughter-in-law, but as her eyes traveled up the expensive and almost transparent rose-colored linen robe to the heavily made-up very young face, she recognized anxiety in Ruth's expression but also something intangible. Naomi looked deeply into the large dark brown eyes which gazed back nervously, and felt an emotion so powerful that her hands unconsciously reached out to the young woman and her face eased into a small smile. "Welcome to the family of Elimelekh of Bethlehem," Naomi said softly in her accented Moabite.

Ruth's face broke into a euphoric smile of joy and she rushed forward to kiss her mother-in-law's hands, as Mahlon unconsciously breathed a sigh of relief.

"Come, let me show you your quarters, and I'll give you a tour of the household. It is not as grand as your father's home, but you will find it quite comfortable, I'm sure. Now we Israelites have a more complicated cooking setup, what with the rules for separating milk and meat..."

Mahlon listened to his mother's voice fading as she led Ruth down the corridor. "That went well," he thought. "Mother will have Ruth as a practicing Israelite before she knows it. But she will have more difficulty with Orpah, from what I have heard from Hilion."

Naomi silently agreed, upon being introduced to Hilion's new wife. Orpah was pleasant enough, and eager to please her new mother-in-law, but the large happy young woman had little sensitivity nor intelligence. She learned to follow Naomi's strict orders about food preparation and the strange Israelite laws of the Sabbath and holiday, but she never could understand the reason behind them nor did she think about the One God. She was just happy being Hilion's wife.

As the years passed, however, and neither Ruth nor Orpah got pregnant, a shadow began to grow over the household, even affecting the ever-contented Orpah. Then one day tragedy struck. A runner rushed into the household informing Naomi that the caravan of her sons had been attacked by Beduin on the way north from Arabia and the two had been killed in the ensuing skirmish.

The household went into deep mourning, and Naomi seemed inconsolable. After the week of sitting on the ground almost silently, Naomi arose and resolutely began organizing the household.

"Mother-in-law, what are you doing? May we help?"

"We are going to sell everything here. We will be returning to Bethlehem."

Both young women began talking at once. Ruth's voice prevailed, as she reminded Naomi that the sale of the household good would have to cover the family debts. She knew that they owed heavily and that the two men had counted on the success of the caravan's goods in the local markets.

"I don't care if I leave with only my clothes on my back. I'm going home!" responded Naomi, and the household was in a flurry of activity for the next few weeks. It turned out that Ruth was accurate in her prediction: once the slaves and household objects and the house itself were sold and the debts repaid, little remained to the three widows. The pieces of silver were carefully wrapped around Naomi's waist, fitted into a thick belt, and the personal jewelry, small vials of perfume, and three or four robes and special sandals were carefully folded and tied into bundles to be carried on the shoulder. The three women were ready, with Ruth and Orpah also carrying water skins, with flat breads, hard cooked eggs, oranges, olives, and dates in a food basket. Few people came to see them off, for over the ten past years the family had less and less to do with its neighbors.

Following the main route north-east, the three women began their long walk, feeling perfectly safe since the highway was patrolled by Moabite soldiers, and then Israelites. They passed caravans along the road, with twenty to thirty heavily laden camels and a hundred or so men walking alongside them. They passed smaller groups leading asses and mules with heavy sacks of grain on their backs. Horsemen in twos and threes cantered past in both directions. On the road it seemed as though everyone was on the move.

The Biblical Woman

The women had started in the cool of daybreak. By midday it was too hot to continue. They found a shady spot off the side of the road and, seated on their bundles, opened the food baskets to share their simple meal.

Orpah's face was red and the sweat was dripping from her upper lip and hairline. She greedily devoured her share of the meal before the other two were even halfway through theirs. Naomi looked at her thoughtfully, and then shifted her focus to Ruth who was daintily breaking off small pieces of bread and popping them into her mouth. Orpah meanwhile leaned back on the trunk of the shade tree and gradually began to doze off. Naomi's thoughtful expression then turned grave and introspective.

With the passage of the heat of midday, the two young women awoke from their naps and began organizing the bundles, but Naomi did not move. Finally, with a deep sigh, she called them over to her. Taking their hands, she turned her face first to one and then to the other:

"Turn back, my daughters. Turn back to Moab and return each of you to your mother's house." Seeing their startled expressions, Naomi grasped their hands even more tightly. "May the Lord deal kindly with you as you have dealt with your dead husbands and with me. I, your mother-in-law, am releasing you from your bond with me and may the Lord grant that each of you finds peace in the home of a new husband." Naomi pulled them to her, and, standing on her toes, kissed Orpah, and then leaned down to kiss Ruth.

The two young women burst into tears and said, "No, no. no. We will return with you to your people!" But Naomi had clearly made up her mind.

"Turn back, my daughters! Why should you go with me? Have I any more sons in my body who might be husband for you according to the law of levirate marriage? Turn back, my daughters, for I am too old to be remarried."

The wailing grew louder and Orpah almost knocked Naomi over as she threw her arms around her. But Naomi had thought through her speech and continued almost woodenly. "Even if I thought there was hope for me, even if I were married tonight, and even if I bore sons, should you wait for them to grow up so as to marry them? Should you live so many years unmarried? Oh no, my daughters! My fate is more bitter than yours for the hand of the Lord has struck at me."

Ruth and Orpah were almost hysterical in their weeping. Then Orpah elbowed Ruth out of the way and grabbed both of Naomi's hands raising them to her lips. She kissed the back of each hand, leaned down to kiss Naomi's two cheeks, and straightening up to full height said:

"You are right, mother-in-law. I bid you farewell and promise that I will never forget you." Turning to Ruth, she embraced her, almost engulfing the smaller woman in her hug. "Farewell Ruth. You have become an Israelite, while I really have not. I am going home." Wiping away her tears, she picked up her bundles, and with a wave, started back to Moab.

"Go, go with her, Ruth!" urged Naomi, but Ruth clung to her. "See, your sister-in-law has returned to her people and to her gods. Go follow Orpah."

"Do not urge me to leave you," replied Ruth. "I will not turn back. Wherever you go, I will go; wherever you lodge, I will lodge; your people are my people, your God is my God." She held Naomi's hands tightly, emphasizing her words with squeezes. "Where you will die, I will die and there I will be buried. Only death will part me from you!"

Naomi stood absolutely still, searching Ruth's face. When she realized how determined Ruth was, she stopped arguing and turned to pick up her bundles. Ruth waited for a sign, and when Naomi stood up with her face wreathed in smiles, she knew that she had won. Smiling in return, Ruth picked up her bundle of clothing and the two women continued on their way.

After a few days, the forbidding scenery of the Dead Sea gradually changed, and the two women turned off the road that led to the coast of the Great Sea through small villages, ever climbing, and Ruth remarked on the varied green colors of the trees and the plants. She noted the small neat fields with the ripening barley. They waved at farmers and were welcomed everywhere with flasks of fresh water and offers of fresh bread and fruit. Gradually the fields became more extensive, and in the distance Ruth saw what seemed to be a city on a hilltop.

"Mother-in-law, what is that large village?" Ruth asked.

Naomi stared into the distance, and with an excited voice said: "That is no village. That is the city of Bethlehem! We are home!" Then in a quieter tone she added: "Home. Now I have to face all the neighbors… I wonder if the house has remained empty all these long years…"

Ruth said nothing, relying totally on Naomi's decision-making as every good daughter-in-law should. She took in everything during the last phase of her journey. She had been practicing her Hebrew, which she had gradually picked up over the years, but she simply could not pronounce some of the vowels the right way. "Well," she thought, "so they will all know that I am a Moabite as soon as I open my mouth. There is nothing I can do. I only hope that they do not dislike strangers and foreigners. She keeps telling me that the Torah orders the Israelites to love strangers, but somehow the many repetitions in the Torah make me a bit suspicious. People are people and here I am the stranger even though I believe as they do."

Despite her misgivings and fears, she was excited and anticipatory. The walls of the city were similar in structure to the Moabite walls, as was the entrance into Bethlehem, with its sharp turn to the left a few feet into the entrance to avoid the high stone wall built to deflect enemy forces. She looked up at the parapets where boiling oil or water could be poured onto enemy soldiers, and took in the low stone structure along the inside of the gate.

"What is this for?" she asked, pointing at the bench-like stones.

"This is where the elders sit in discussion and judgement," responded Naomi, "and where anyone may rest in the shade." Her eyes were not on her daughter-in-law, however, but on a group of young and middle aged women gathered near the well in the open square beyond the gate. She saw the glances toward her, and then the startled stares. One older woman slowly came toward them, followed by the others who walked even more slowly.

"Can this be Naomi?" she asked. At the nod, the women all rushed forward, surrounding her and buzzing with excitement.

"Do not call me Naomi, which means pleasantness. Call me "Mara" or bitterness, for the Lord has made my lot very bitter." The women listened respectfully. "I went away full –with husband and two sons—and the Lord has brought me back empty, for all three have died. I am full of misfortune."

The women looked on sympathetically, clucking over her misfortunes. Then one of the younger women said:

"And who is this?" pointing at Ruth.

"My daughter-in-law Ruth who has chosen of her own free will to come to Judea with me," responded Naomi, pulling Ruth into the center of the circle of women. "Her act of loving kindness should be known from the start." She affectionately placed her arm around Ruth's shoulders. "Now, tell me, is my husband's home awaiting us?"

"Oh yes, Naomi. No one moved in to any of the homes left during the famine. We always took it for granted that you who left would some day return."

They accompanied Naomi and Ruth to the large house, built in the wealthy section of the city. That evening and for some time after, the townspeople stopped by to share their milk, cheese, olives, fruit, and bread. Slowly the two women cleaned up their living quarters and the overgrown interior garden, but Naomi said to leave the main sections of the large house alone, as they were only two women without slaves or servant or men. Ruth took on the task of drawing water from the main well, but although the other women nodded and smiled at her, none befriended her.

One day, a few weeks after their arrival, on her return from fetching the morning water, Ruth hesitantly addressed Naomi:

"Mother-in-law…I see young men and women leaving for the barley harvest, very early in the morning. You have taught me that our Torah has laws to help the poor. You taught me that the poor may walk after the harvesters and glean the fallen stalks of grain for their own use." Seeing Naomi's facial expression pushed Ruth the quickly state the rest of her case.

"Mother-in-law, we have waited almost a month for your husband's near kin to come forth to buy up his land from you, since widows do not inherit in Israel. But no one has come to do this. We have no money, we have almost no food. Please, please, allow me to go to the fields and glean."

She looked pleadingly at Naomi who, with a sigh, said, "Ruth, you are so wise and so generous. Yes, Elimelekh's kin are ignoring their duty to redeem his land. Unfortunately, custom forbids me to confront them or even to go to the town elders. Well, perhaps we can shame them into action by openly declaring our poverty to the entire town. And we do have to eat." Sighing again, she carefully went over the laws of gleaning, reminding Ruth that she could not touch the sheaves tied up in the fields by the harvesters, nor could she pick stalks that the scythes had missed; she could only do the backbreaking work of bending over to pick up each separate fallen and forgotten stalk.

"And Ruth, it is very hot in the fields. Remember to drink much water and rest from time to time in the shade. You are not used to physical work."

As Ruth prepared to leave, Naomi also added another word of caution: "Keep your head covered at all times, not just to keep out the dust, but to prevent sunstroke. Goodby, farewell. May you have good luck today."

Naomi turned back into the house, as Ruth hurried down the road, through the city gate, and out into the fields.

"Which one shall I enter?" thought Ruth as she came upon the reapers. "That field looks as though it has enough gleaners. I'll go on a bit to find a less crowded one."

Ruth walked past the next five or six fields. Then ahead she saw one that only had a handful of gleaners. Shyly she approached the overseer and waited to be noticed. As he turned to look in her direction, she politely asked him: "Please, sir, let me glean and gather among the sheaves behind the reapers."

The overseer looked her up and down, recognizing the accent as Moabite. "Certainly, daughter-in-law of Naomi," he said. "Just follow along with the other gleaners."

Ruth smiled her thanks and hurried over to the others. All morning she worked, remembering to drink from her skin of water. By midmorning, as the sun became very strong, she listened to the others and went to rest in the shade of the lean-to, but went back to the field as soon as she could. As she worked she noticed a lone rider approach from the direction of Bethlehem. He dismounted, and one of the reapers hurried up to take the reins and lead the handsome horse into the shade.

"Aha," thought Ruth. "The owner of these fields has arrived…What is his name again? Oh yes, Boaz." She watched him surveying the fields, and when she felt him looking at her, she quickly averted her eyes and continued working. Out of the corner of her eye she saw Boaz conversing with his overseer, and then walking. In a panic, she realized he was headed toward her. She pretended not to notice, but he placed himself directly in her path so that she had to stand up and face him.

"Listen to me, daughter," Boaz said in his deep kind voice. "Don't go to glean in another field, but stay here, close to the young women who usually glean here. Keep your eyes on the field they are reaping and follow them. I have ordered my young men not to molest you." Ruth's eyes opened wide at this and she looked at Boaz's face for the first time. He smiled at her and continued: "And when you are thirsty, go to the big jars and drink from that water which is cooler and more plentiful than what you brought with you from home."

Ruth, forgetting her Israelite manners, prostrated herself with her face to the ground, as good Moabite women did to their masters. "Why are you so kind as to single me out, when I am a foreigner?" she asked, her voice breaking in emotion.

"Please arise, daughter-in-law of Naomi. I have been told of all that you did for Naomi after the death of your husband, how you left your father and mother and birthplace and came to a people you had not known before. May the Lord reward your deeds." Boaz looked into Ruth's eyes and added, "May you have full recompense from the Lord of Israel under whose wings you have sought refuge."

Ruth answered as modesty dictated: "you are most kind, my lord, to comfort me and to speak gently to your servant, though," she hastened to add, "I am not so much as one of your servants." With that, she turned back to her work.

At the hottest time of the day, the young women told Ruth to join them all at the lean-to for they took time out to eat. She left her bundle of gleanings with a shawl on top of it, as she saw the others do. Then she headed for the shade. Temporarily blinded upon entering the shelter, she found herself facing Boaz who, smiling at her, said: "Come over here and partake of the meal. Here," he said as she sat, passing a small clay bowl filled with liquid to her, "dip your bread in the vinegar. It will refresh you." Ruth did so, and after the shock of the acid taste subsided, she felt her mouth come alive and she ate with appetite. Boaz watched her eat and passed another small bowl to her, this one filled with roasted grain. Ruth hungrily ate her fill, and had some left over. Boaz tactfully looked the other way, and Ruth poured the remaining grain into a small square of cloth which she tied to her empty water skin.

When she got up to continue gleaning, Boaz waited until she was out of earshot and then gave orders to his workers. "You are not only to let her glean among the sheaves without interference, but you are also to pull some stalks from the heaps and leave them for her. Do not scold her." The men obeyed their master, who watched the work from a distance, then remounted his horse and slowly and thoughtfully returned to the city.

Ruth worked until evening. Then she beat out her gleaning, thus removing the grainhead from the stalk—for which she had no use since she had no animals to feed—and placed the barley in a large rectangle of cloth, tying it up into a bundle weighing about an *ephah*. Placing it on her shoulder, and collecting her belongings from the lean-to, she started to climb uphill to Bethlehem arriving as the last of the light faded from the sky. Naomi saw her coming and rushed out to greet her.

"Come, come. No talking, not until you have eaten the hot soup I have ready for you." While Ruth ate, Naomi unpacked the bundles including the small one containing the roasted grain, and turned to Ruth in astonishment. "Where did you glean today? Where did you work? Blessed be he who took such generous notice of you." Naomi knew that there was too much in the bundles for it to be a normal daily amount of gleanings.

By this time, Ruth had finished eating and drinking. While washing up, she told Naomi every detail of her day, especially of her meeting Boaz. Naomi exclaimed: "Blessed be he, for he is related to my husband. He is one of the redeemers of our land. So stay with his young women as he told you. Perhaps he will take action over the redemption of the land."

So Ruth arose early every morning, before daybreak, and set out on the walk to the barley fields. She worked until the barley harvest was over, returning every night to Naomi despite the constant invitations to sleep in the fields. Ruth knew that Naomi needed her company and her food; she also did not want there to be any gossip about her in the city, where everyone talked about everyone.

The wheat harvest followed the festival of Shavuot and Ruth had to walk even farther to Boaz's wheat fields. They had been in Bethlehem for many months and nothing had been done to redeem Elimelekh's land. Naomi thought about this long and hard, and finally, at the end of the wheat harvest, spoke to Ruth.

"Daughter, sit here with me," Naomi said, patting the space on the low couch next to her. "I must seek a home for you where you will be happy." She stilled Ruth's protest before it started. "I have a plan, and may I remind you that I am still the matriarch in this household." Ruth inclined her head, and Naomi continued.

"You have worked in our kinsman Boaz's fields. He will be winnowing grain on his threshing floor tonight. So I want you to bathe, anoint yourself with the expensive oils from your marriage portion, dress up in your fine linen robe, and go to the threshing floor. Wait, wait, hear me out. I have thought this through. Do not let Boaz see you, but mark where he lies down after eating and drinking. In this land, winnowing is a time of celebration and wine is consumed. The land owner remains in the threshing area partly to discourage theft and partly to celebrate with his workers."

"When Boaz is asleep and all is quiet, you are to go over and uncover the blanket from his feet and lie down there." Ruth looked at Naomi with complete trust and did not question a thing that she had been told to do, although is must have sounded bizarre. "Boaz will tell you what you are to do."

Ruth nodded. "I will do everything you tell me." She proceeded with her bath, dressed and perfumed herself, and set out for the threshing floor which was located next to the barley fields. Covered with a cloak, she stood almost unnoticed at the edge of the festive activities, watching the men holding the large sieve and throwing the grain high in the air where the evening wind could blow away the chaff covering the grain. Once this was done, the finished grain was emptied into storage bins and the next batch of raw grain was placed on the sieve to be winnowed, until all the grain had been thus treated.

The workers ate and drank what the women served and there was a general merriment until gradually everyone fell asleep rolled up in their blankets or cloaks. Ruth noted where Boaz lay, just as the last of the fires was doused. When all around her came sounds of deep breathing or snoring, Ruth stealthily picked her way over to Boaz, uncovered his feet, and lay down, just as Naomi had told her to do. But she did not sleep.

In the middle of the night, Boaz turned over in his sleep and stretched his feet, touching softness where should not have been softness. Startled, he awoke completely, and pulling back his cover, smelled the perfume of a woman lying at his feet.

"Who are you?" he whispered.

"I am your servant Ruth. Spread you robe over me for you are a redeeming kinsman." Ruth did not know where the words came from and until that point had not consciously known of her decision to connect herself to the redemption of the land. But after having spoken this way to Boaz, Ruth felt satisfied with her decision. She awaited Boaz's response with bated breath.

It was as though Boaz had stopped breathing, as the full import of Ruth's statement registered in his mind. As the implications, both legal and personal, became crystal clear, he almost cried with joy, that he, in his middle years, should attract a woman as young and as noble as Ruth. He had refused to consciously entertain such thoughts ever since he had met her. But while her actions forced him to act, he also knew that there was one major hurdle to overcome.

"Be blessed of the Lord, my daughter! Your latest deed of loyalty is greater than the first. Your first was to stay with your mother-in-law; your latest is still directed toward her for in choosing to connect yourself to the redemption of the land, you will provide her with a spiritual grandchild. You flatter me that you have not turned to younger men, neither rich nor poor."

Boaz could make out Ruth's face in the moonlight and what he saw pleased him.

"Now, my daughter—and I call you that because you are so much younger than I am—fear not. I will do on your behalf what you ask, for all the elders of the town know what a fine woman you are. But, while it is true that I am a redeeming kinsman, there is another redeemer closer than I and thus he has first option on Elimelekh's land. So, stay the night, and in the morning I will act as the law demands. If he will act as a redeemer, good!"

Boaz saw Ruth's horrified look, for she knew to whom he referred and certainly did not want to marry him. He took her hand, so small in both of his, and calmed her by adding:

"But if he refuses to act as redeemer for you, Ruth, I will do so myself. I promise!" He watched her relax and with complete faith in him and in God's plans, Ruth lay down at Boaz's feet, but did not sleep. At dawn, before one person could distinguish another, Ruth rose to leave. Boaz leaped up, agreeing with her unspoken desire not to be seen at the threshing floor and thus open to gossip. He went to the huge pile of grain and whispered: "Hold out your shawl that you are wearing."

Ruth opened it up to full size and Boaz measured out six measures of grain and helped her tie it up and put it on her back. "This is for Naomi as a promise of a brideswealth to come. You should not return to her empty-handed."

Ruth walked back home in a daze of excitement and expectation. She knew that Naomi would explain everything to her, which Naomi did, trying not to show her own excitement and nervousness.

"Stay here, Ruth, until you learn how the matter turns out. Boaz must act today and once he acts, the issue will be settled. May the Lord bless us all."

Ruth learned the details of the redeeming of the land after the event. Boaz had gone to the gate of the city and sat on the bench-like stones to await the first redeemer, Elimelekh's closest male relative. Boaz knew that he would eventually pass through the gate on his way to his fields. Meanwhile, the townspeople saw Boaz sitting there and knew that something was about to happen, for Boaz had never done this before. Thus there was an audience when Ploni Almoni sauntered down the hill from his house heading to the gate.

"Come over and sit down here!" called Boaz to his relative in a no-nonsense voice. As soon as he was seated, Boaz motioned to ten of the town elders, who had been hovering around curiously, to be seated as well. This was a court of judgment, and the people pushed close to watch and listen.

Boaz stated to Ploni Almoni: "Naomi, recently returned from the land of Moab, must sell her husband's land to his nearest relative, for, as you know, widows may not inherit but may live off of the price of the redemption of the land. It is your right to redeem the land first, although why you have not acquired it until now and fulfilled your obligation, I do not know."

The man began to protest, but Boaz silenced him and continued: "You are brought before the elders to act here and now. If you are willing to redeem the land, redeem! But if you will not, tell me, for I come after you and I will do so."

"I am willing to redeem it," replied the man. But Boaz was not finished.

"When you acquire the property from Naomi and from Ruth, you must also acquire Ruth for she has freely chosen to perpetuate the name of her dead husband."

The townspeople gasped for although levirate marriage was mandatory for a childless widow and a brother-in-law, it was not mandatory if there was no brother of the dead man. Boaz and the townspeople faced Ploni Almoni, whose face reflected his conflicting emotions. He could just picture his rich wife's reaction to his coming home with a young widow as a second wife. She would probably leave him and take all her wealth with her, for upper class women could do so according to prenuptial agreements. Also, Ruth was a Moabite. Didn't it say in the Torah that you couldn't marry a Moabite? Too bad he had never paid too much attention to his lessons...

"Then I cannot redeem the land, lest I impair my own estate," he blurted out, and turning to Boaz he said, "you may take over my right of redemption, for I am unable to exercise it."

Boaz had counted on Ploni Almon's ignorance of Jewish law as a factor in his rejection of Ruth, for it was only male Moabites that were forbidden, not the women. He also knew of his relative's overbearing and possessive wife. Even so, he had been very nervous as the thought of the possibility of losing Ruth just as he had found her.

The court of elders then supervised the formal act of passing the power of the redemption of the land from one relative to the next. The closest relative had to remove his sandal and hand it over, publicly, to the next relative, as a symbolic act of severing his claim. This done, Boaz proclaimed to the elders and to the crowd gathered in the square:

"You are all witnesses today that I am acquiring from Naomi all that belonged to Elimelekh, Chilion, and Mahlon. I am also acquiring Ruth the Moabite, wife of Mahlon, as my wife, so as to perpetuate the name of the deceased. You are all witnesses!"

"We are witnesses!" the townspeople formally responded, and then with great excitement at the event, one of the leaders stated: "May the Lord make the woman who is coming into your house like Rahel and Leah, both of whom built up the family of Israel." Another leader shouted: "May your clan of Ephrat prosper and may your name be perpetuated in Bethlehem!" A third added: "May your home be like that of Peretz whom Tamar bore to Judah, through the children which the Lord will give you by this young woman!"

Jubilantly Boaz went up to Naomi's house to inform her and Ruth of the events and to set the marriage date in three days' time. The town's women set about preparing the food for the feast, each contributing something, the large house was cleaned from top to bottom, the musical instruments were tuned, and the bride was bathed, anointed, combed, and dressed. All of Bethlehem participated in the wedding, and when Ruth was led to Boaz by Naomi, there wasn't a dry eye in the crowd. So Boaz married Ruth and the Lord blessed them with fertility, so that after all those years Ruth finally had a son. The women who helped with the birthing said to Naomi: "Blessed be the Lord who has given you a redeemer today. May his name be perpetuated in Israel."

"The baby will renew your life and sustain your old age, for he is yours through the action of Ruth who remains your daughter-in-law through her act of love and compassion," added a second woman.

"She loves you and is better to you than seven sons." Added a third woman. "Truly a son is born to Naomi."

Naomi took the baby and held it close. Ruth watched tiredly and contentedly from her bed. The two women smiled at each other and Naomi said to the baby, "Oved, we will call you Oved at your circumcision."

Boaz entered the room to see his son and his wife. "I have great plans for him," he said, and they all laughed, and dreamed their own private dreams.

Notes

The Biblical text for this chapter is the Scroll of Ruth.

For background material, I recommend William Stiebing, *Ancient Near Eastern History and Culture* (Routledge, 2016); Ephraim Stern, *The Material Culture of the Land of the Bible* (Aris & Phillips, 1982); Philip King and Lawrence E. Stager, *Life in Biblical Israel* (Westminster John Knox Press, 2001); and Jennie R. Ebeling, *Women's Lives in Biblical Times* (T & T Clark International, 2010), chapters 2, 4, 5, and 7.

Chana

The midwife crouched below the birthing woman who leaned back on the stool screaming in pain.

"Come on, come on," she crooned. "Once more and it will be out."

The woman took a deep breath and all the women around her seemed to do the same. She bore down as the sweat rolled down her face soaking the already damp linen shirt. The infant emerged and everyone began cheering, clucking, and ululating at the same time. Everyone except one woman who had been standing near the door of the room. She turned and stumbled out, heading almost blindly through the open courtyard into the vineyard on the other side of the family compound. She ran and ran until she reached the far side of the vineyard, where she stopped to catch her breath. She gulped for air while crying almost hysterically.

"Why, why, why?" she intoned. "This is her fourth child. Four, four, four. And I have none. None, none, none." With her arms wrapped around herself for warmth, Chana stood there in her misery, oblivious to the beauty of the night. Much later she slowly climbed back to the house, and slipped silently into her room, closing the door after her. She was startled to hear her husband's voice coming from the direction of her bed, for the room was dark.

"I was worried about you," Elkana said.

"Don't worry about me," Chana replied.

"I did not see you in Penina's room when I came in to look at the new baby."

"Why should I stay there to see her gloating face?"

"Now, Chana, Penina doesn't gloat."

"So what do you call it?"

"She's merely proud of birthing and surviving."

"She's gloating because I am barren."

"Your time will come."

"When? When? When I'm forty?"

"When God chooses." Elkana tried to comfort Chana but she was too miserable to respond. "Am I not better to you than ten sons? You know how much I love you."

Chana allowed herself to relax a bit but in her mind she thought, "No, you're not. I want a child!" Her thoughts drifted back in time. Fifteen years ago, and it seemed like yesterday as well as an eternity. Elkana's father and her father had met to discuss the marriage of their children. They were cousins and so had seen each other from time to time as they were growing up. Chana had always liked his serious demeanor and he had been attracted by her sensitivity. He had helped her put a baby bird back in is nest after she had seen the mother bird frantically flapping here and there. He had survived the pecking and had been rewarded with Chana's enchanting smile of thanks.

Their marriage had seemed inevitable, and as the two patriarchs announced the conclusion of negotiations, the women rushed to bring in the fruit, almonds, dried raisins and figs, and wine to celebrate. The brideswealth was not considered too onerous although it was large enough as honor demanded, for it meant merely shifting clan wealth from one part of the huge family to the other.

The wedding had taken place on time and Chana had begun her new life as optimistically as any other young Israelite woman. She even got along with her mother-in-law, at least at the beginning. But then month after month, while all the other new brides began to show large bellies, Chana did not get pregnant. At first it did not bother her, for she knew that many fourteen-year-olds were not yet ready to be mothers. But as the months stretched into years, and she heard whispers of sympathy around her in the woman's quarters and in the marketplace, Chana became concerned. She gradually felt that her mother-in-law's attitude was changing. When she mentioned this to Elkana, he remained silent.

"What is it Elkana? Your mother no longer looks directly at me when she talks to me. It is as though I am becoming a non-person." She looked him in the eyes and the pain that she saw there shocked her.

"What is it, my husband?" she whispered. "You know that you can tell me anything."

"Chana, my beloved, my mother has given me a direct order that pains me to my soul." He earnestly looked at her and took her cold hands in his. She shivered in anticipation of bad news. "We have been married almost five years now and have not produced a child." He took a deep breath and continued. "My mother told me that I must either divorce you or take another wife so as to determine who is at fault."

Chana sat there like a statue. Divorce or a co-wife. She could not live without Elkana, so deep was her love for him. But could she share him? Some of her friends were co-wives, and most were relatively harmonious. In fact, some co-wives were very affectionate with each other, treating each other's children with love. Others were not so lucky. What would her fate be? From a distance she heard her husband's voice.

"Chana, what is your wish? Do you want to return to your father's home and marry a man of his choice or do you prefer to remain with me and take the chance that my mother's choice of another wife will work out well? Chana, talk to me."

Looking down at her hands which were tightly clasped in her husband's, Chana slowly replied: "I would never leave you of my own free will, Elkana, for you are the sun and the moon to me. I will submit to your mother's will and hope against hope that your new wife will be loving, generous," and with a tremulous voice she added, "and fertile."

Elkana enveloped his tiny wife in a bear-hug, and the two cried together in the privacy of their rooms. "I will tell mother of our decision in the morning."

Within five months the wedding had taken place. Chana had stayed out of sight, and this suited her mother-in-law well, for she did not dislike her daughter-in-law, and in fact sympathized; but practicality had to reign supreme and Elkana had to have children. Love had no place in such decision making, thought his mother as she bustled about supervising the whitewashing of the co-wife's rooms at the other end of the general sleeping quarters. As soon as that would be completed, the slaves would come in to construct a low, wooden frame for the bed, a simple affair consisting of four legs lashed with thick hemp to four boards. The boards would then have thick flat hemp straps attached with pegs, then interwoven to form an understructure for the thick wool fleece-stuffed colorful mattresses to be brought by the new bride. Elkana's mother reminded the slaves to make sure that there were no unwanted insects, and especially snakes and scorpions, hiding in the corner where the bed would be placed.

Mentally blessing the nameless inventor of the bed platform, Elkana's mother ordered the slaves to bring in the carved wooden chest which had belonged to her mother, to serve as a place where the new bride could keep her personal things. Two colorful woven carpets added the last touch, then the room was ready. The wedding was set for the next day and Elkana's mother went on to supervise the preparation of their share of the food to be served. She caught a glimpse of Chana down the corridor, and her heart filled with momentary sympathy for her charming sensitive daughter-in-law, but it passed and she went about her business.

Chana had spent the night of Elkana's second wedding out in the olive orchard. In the early hours of the morning, when the dew had made her robe sodden, she tip-toed back to her apartment, removing the wet clothing and shivering as she got under the woven woolen blanket in a fresh night robe. She did not think that she could sleep, but an overwhelming yawn overtook her and she drifted off.

Chana's first meeting with Penina did not go well. Penina disdainfully looked her up and down as if to say there was no reason for her to have anything to fear from the rivalry of such a tiny skinny woman. After all, Penina was plump and broad, perfect for comfort and child bearing. Chana tried to be friendly, but each time she was rebuffed. She glanced at her mother-in-law and caught her thoughtfully frowning as she looked at Penina.

Elkana soon found himself in the role of peace maker. He did not know which wife to believe at first. On the one hand he knew that Chana would not lie, but on the other hand he knew that she was terribly upset about having to share her life with a co-wife. Then he heard Penina complaining about Chana's behavior and he was unsure of her truthfulness because Penina cried so easily and cuddled up to him so trustingly. Finally he went to speak to his mother, who after trying diplomatically to get out of giving a direct answer, looked him in the eyes and said:

"Elkana, I thought I had chosen well, but Penina is obviously a manipulator who is attempting to displace Chana completely. You and I are going to have to try to cope with this rivalry because there is no going back. As a matter of fact, I think that Penina is already with child."

She was right on all counts, and as the years passed life did not become easier for any of them. Penina had one child after another, flaunting her fertility in front of Chana as well as her mother-in-law. She also grew rounder from year to year. The children were told to avoid Chana who was willing to share in their raising, but Penina would have none of this.

Chana, however, retained Elkana's love, and aside from the times that he had to be with Penina to fulfill his marital obligations to her, Elkana spent his time with Chana. He thought she was becoming too thin, but when he said something to her, she laughingly rejected his statement by pointing out that she remained the same, but Penina kept getting heavier and heavier.

The two women were supervised by Elkana's mother but as the years passed she gave more control over to Chana, explaining to Penina that the latter had to focus on her growing family's demands. Chana was thus inducted into the matriarchal supervisory powers, such as checking the supplies of grain, flour grinding, the supply of olive oil and nut oil, the quantity of raisins, dates, figs, the preparation of the fresh foods, and finally, the supervision of the slaves who cleaned and baked and sewed and spun and wove. Chana's life was thus a busy one.

From year to year, at the time of one of the three pilgrimage festivals, Elkana would gather his wives and children and travel the distance to Shilo. His favorite holiday was Succot, in the early autumn, when he had harvested all of his fruit and felt particularly grateful to God for the harvest. Chana was in charge of the details of the pilgrimage, and she looked forward to the excitement of the trip, and the hustle and bustle of the city along with the ritual visit to the Sanctuary to offer up the big animals to the Lord.

The only negative aspect to the pilgrimage was that it brought with it the physically close sharing of small quarters with Penina and the children. They usually rented two rooms from a resident of Shilo who was related to Elkana, but now with four children along, two rooms would be very cramped. Penina also seemed to think that it was her right to be waited on, even by a co-wife. Oh well, sighed Chana, she would just have to bear it. It was a small thing to suffer in order to be able to go to God's dwelling.

It was time! The donkeys were saddled for the women and children, and the sheep and goats for the offerings were roped together. The pack mule was laden with all the food and clothing for the trip, and the skins filled with water were placed on each side of the donkeys' necks. Elkana would purchase the palm and citron in Shilo. The myrtle and willows he had picked from his own garden, carefully wrapping them in a damp cloth. The sun was just rising as the small party set off for Shilo; they should arrive the next day, thus having to sleep only one night in a farmhouse along the way.

Chana felt a surge of excitement as they started off. The holidays of Rosh Ha-Shana and Yom Kippur were over and the summer heat had disappeared. The hills were carefully planted and the grapevines were still very green, as were the fruit trees. Farmers waved at them as they passed, and women came forward to offer water and to walk alongside chatting and exchanging news. Everyone was feeling good and the tight quarters of the farmer's house that first night were bearable because all of the exhausted children and adults fell asleep immediately after a light supper of bread, cheese, olives, and water. Elkana slipped out to make sure that the animals were all resting well.

Early the next day the ride continued, and before noon they spotted Shilo on the mountainside. More and more people were riding and walking as they neared the city. The noise level rose as did the dust and by the time they arrived at the cousin's compound, the children were cranky and squabbling. When they were escorted to their small two-room apartment, Penina complained loudly that there was not enough space for her and the four children. Looking balefully at Chana who was busy organizing the unloading of the food, cookware, and bedding, she loudly said to Elkana: "I want the bigger room this time. She doesn't need so much space. She's only one person, one small person, and we are five."

Chana stopped in the middle of her task and said, "And should I also move all the food, bedding, and animals in with me, to the inner room?"

"Please Chana, please Penina. The reason you get the inner room is partly to make sure of where the children are and partly because Chana takes care of all the cooking and public duties that can only take place in the front room."

"Then I will do those things while we are here. I want the larger room this time."

"You, cook? You, organize? The only thing you know how to do…" Chana stopped.

"Yes," sneered Penina, "the only thing I know how to do is what you can't do and never will be able to do."

"That's all!" reprimanded Elkana. "Take the children in there, and wash them. By that time Chana will have supper ready." Sulking, Penina pushed the bigger ones ahead of her, unwrapping the baby from the large kerchief wrapped around her chest which had held him in place while freeing her hands during the journey.

Chana's mood was ruined. She mechanically prepared the meal, served it, ate her portion, cleaned up, and went to bed. Sleep deserted her as she heard Penina's taunting over and over in her head. Her bad mood continued into the next day when Elkana took one of the sheep over to the Sanctuary to offer it up to the Lord. The priests slaughtered the animal, cut out the portion to be burned on the altar to God, removed a share for them, and returned the rest of the slaughtered animal to Elkana which he then proceeded to bring back to the living quarters where the meat was skewered and broiled over an open fire in the family compound courtyard.

The smell was delicious. The only time they ate red meat was after these offerings, and the children watched the procedure with anticipation. When the roasting was completed, Elkana divided out a portion to each member of the family, but to Chana he gave a double portion. She looked the meat in her ceramic bowl but could not eat it. Her depression was overwhelming.

Penina devoured her meat with appetite, gloating silently over Chana's mood. She and the children left the eating area immediately after finishing, the older ones eyeing Chana's uneaten portion questioningly.

"Please Chana, please eat," said Elkana softly when they were alone. "I know that it still pains you to be childless. But am I not better than ten sons?"

His concern broke through her fog of self-pity, but Chana simply could not eat. She picked at her portion, pretending, but in the end gave it back to Elkana. "Maybe tomorrow," she said as she rose to clear the area.

The next morning, after a long sleepless night full of terrifying dreams, Chana felt desperate. She found herself drawn to the Sanctuary, retracing her steps of the previous day when she had accompanied Elkana to give the offerings. But this time she came along and empty-handed.

Chana barely noticed Eli, the high priest, who was seated at the main entrance of the Sanctuary, visually checking all who entered and left. Chana found herself momentarily blinded by the stark contrast between the shady interior and the bright sunshine outside the Sanctuary. Blinking automatically, Chana discovered that she was blinking back tears at the same time. Facing the Holy of Holies, hidden behind the separating curtain, Chana felt the emotions and bitterness of the past few years spilling out of her mouth in a verbalization of her subconscious thoughts.

"Please, Oh Lord, please heed your unworthy servant. Send me a child, a male child, and I will return him to you as soon as he is weaned, to become part of Your Sanctuary here in Shilo. He will be a temporary loan to me, and furthermore, I take an oath that he shall be a Nazirite all of his life, never drinking wine and never cutting his hair, as proof of Your glory."

Chana spilled her vexation out to the Lord, her lips moving but no sound emerging. She was so wrapped up in her bargaining with God that she did not hear Eli the high priest walk up to her, watching her with an enraged expression on his usually kind face.

"Drunken woman! How dare you enter the house of the Lord full of wine!"

Startled, Chana's eyes focused on Eli. "No, no my lord," she replied. "I am not drunk, but I spoke to the Lord from the innermost part of my being."

Eli looked at the sensitive face, pale and drawn, and realized his error. The tiny woman before him was almost shivering despair and embarrassment. "I am sorry, so sorry to have accused you, but I saw your lips moving and heard no sound; therefore I thought you a drunk. Well, well…now I know the reason for such strange actions…" Chana stood before him, barely reaching his shoulder, looking like a terrified wild bird. "May the Lord grant you that which you begged for," Eli added, watching with astonishment as Chana's face began to glow in anticipation of this happening. He watched her take a deep breath, as though invigorated and full of hope. "Oh my," Eli thought, "she thinks that now it will come true because of the platitude I just said. Well, why not? If she believes it, and I helped a little, who knows if that isn't God's way?!"

"Good day, my lord," said Chana sweetly, "and thank you from the bottom of my heart for your blessing." She turned on her heel heading out of the main opening with a youthful spring to her walk.

"Go with God," mumbled Eli, "and may you really receive what you so badly desire."

Chana returned to the rented quarters in wonderful spirits. Elkana met her as she turned into the central entrance to the compound. "Chana," he rushed forward. "you had me so worried! You were gone before I awoke…Chana you look wonderful! What happened?" He looked at her happy face in astonishment. She had not looked this elated in years. But Chana merely smiled a private smile, patted him on the hand, and set about preparing the holiday meal. This time when Elkana gave her a double portion, she consumed it all with appetite. She even smiled at a perplexed Penina who kept glancing at her suspiciously. The mood continued until after the two-day return trip home, at the conclusion of the festival.

"Ah, it is so good to go away," said Elkana upon entering his home, "but it is even better to return home." His mother came out to greet them all, telling them that the baths were ready along with fresh clothing and a hot meal. Noting Chana's cheerful disposition, she remarked, "Well, Chana. This pilgrimage seems to have done you some good. It's good to see you happy again."

Chana just smiled and went about her business. The tension in the entire household eased with these smiles. Only Penina did not trust them, instinctively sensing that it boded badly for her. She was right, for about three months later while Elkana's mother was working alongside Chana supervising the laundering of the family's linens, she looked at Chana's profile and looked again more closely.

"Chana, Chana. Come here my dear." Surprised, Chana stopped in the midst of her work and stepped over. Her mother-in-law took Chana's face in her hands, tears misting her eyes. "You're with child, you're finally with child!"

Touching her belly almost with awe, Chana silently nodded, "Yes, God has been kind."

"You should rest more and be careful not to lift heavy things, and you must eat rich fatty things to make the baby healthy, and.." she stopped her listing when she heard Chana's light giggle. She smiled and said, "but you know all this. I'm only concerned. And happy. Very happy." She hugged Chana, oblivious to the jealous looks coming from Penina's direction and to the mumbled complaint, "…you never hugged me like that with any of my pregnancies."

The days and weeks and months passed rapidly for Chana. Elkana was elated but at the same time he knew that Chana was hiding something. As the time for birthing drew near, Chana went for a slow walk with Elkana in the grape arbor. The smell of the ripening grapes was intoxicating and the stars twinkled as they did on all crisp clear night in the land of Israel.

"Go on," he said, "tell me what has been on your mind all this time."

"Oh, Elkana, I should have known that you would guess." Chana took a deep breath and blurted out the entire story of her experience in the Sanctuary, the bargain she had made with God, and the vow to turn the boy child—if it were a boy—over to the Lord as a Nazirite. "And then the High Priest himself blessed me, Elkana. Please do not negate my vow even though it is within you patriarchal powers to do so. I know that the baby is also yours, but the Lord listened to my plea because of my unselfishness. Please Elkana, please."

Elkana stood at the edge of the arbor, automatically plucked a leaf from a nearby tree and began shredding it. Then he turned to his very round wife. He could see the concern and hope on her face even in the dim light.

"Chana, if after all these years of childlessness you can tolerate giving up your son to God's service, who am I to stand in your way. I waive my right to negate your vow and if it is a boy, we will both deliver him to Eli at Shilo."

"Thank you, my husband."

"Give me you hand and let's climb the hill to return home. Slowly, Chana, for your time is near."

"If I get any bigger, I think I will explode."

Laughing at the idea, the two returned to the house where a few hours later Chana awoke urgently telling Elkana to fetch his mother. "It's coming. Fast and hard. Go Elkana, I do not want you to hear my cries."

He left quickly, and all the women gathered, each doing her share to ease the birth.

"She's so tiny," the midwife said.

"But strong and determined," said Elkana's mother.

"I can't believe that she does not yell nor curse her husband."

"She has waited years and years for this."

"Here it comes! It's a boy, a strong boy with an enormous voice."

"Call Elkana!"

Elkana entered, hesitantly approaching Chana's bed. There she lay, holding her new son all bundled in swaddling clothes, face shining with joy.

"Let's name him Samuel, because I asked the Lord for him and the Lord lent him to us." Elkana nodded in agreement and eight days later, at the circumcision, that became the baby's name.

Chana's life became focused around her son's feeding patterns, and when Elkana mentioned getting ready for the annual autumn pilgrimage, she begged off going, saying, "I will go when Samuel is weaned, for when we all go and he appears for the first time at the Sanctuary, he must remain there forever."

Elkana gave her permission to remain behind although he would miss her company. She quietly celebrated the festival with her mother-in-law, eating roasted pigeons instead of roasted lamb or kid.

Samuel grew into a strapping boy, nursing noisily, but gradually eating solid food as well. Chana sang to him little songs that she composed on the spot, and Samuel, learning to talk, sang along with her. At about the age of three, he overheard his mother reciting something that he could not completely understand as she worked her spinning and weaving.

"Ima, what are you saying? Is it a song like the one about the birds praising the Lord?" he asked.

"No, Samuel. This is a private song of praise that I have been composing ever since you were born."

"Sing it to me!"

"It is not really sung. It's more like a chant."

"Chant it to me!"

Chana looked at her intelligent and sensitive son. "All right. You may not understand it all yet, but you will eventually." To the rhythm of the shuttle on the loom, Chana recited:

> My heart exults in the Lord:
> I have triumphed through the Lord
> I gloat over my enemies
> I rejoice in Your deliverance.
> There is no Holy One like the Lord,
> Truly, there is none beside you;
> There is no rock like our God.
> Talk no more with lofty pride,
> Let no arrogance cross your lips.
> For the Lord is an all-knowing God,
> By Him actions are measured .

She stopped both her weaving and her chanting, deep in thought.

"Is there more, Ima? It's easy to understand. Repeat it so that I can chant with you."

"Yes," she replied, "there is more but I haven't finished finding the right words yet." She resumed her weaving, patiently repeating with Samuel the section she had completed. A few weeks later, Samuel was helping in the vegetable garden, and he began to chant Chana's song. Elkana stopped working, listening carefully.

"Samuel, is that your mother's poetry?"

"Of course, father. I'm too little to compose my own. And it's not finished."

"Will you sing me the next part when you learn it?"

"Of course, but it's not a song. It's a chant."

When the family prepared for the next pilgrimage, Samuel was anxious to go too.

"Why not us, Ima? Penina's baby is younger than I am and he's going."

"We will go next year Samuel. Meanwhile when we will be alone, I'll teach you the rest of my song."

"But why can't I go too. And you can teach it to me while we ride."

"Samuel, when we go to Shilo, you are going to stay there with Eli the High Priest and all the Kohanim."

"Yes, I know. I'm going to go to school and learn to read and write the holy scriptures. And then I'll come home for my meals and I'll teach you what I learn."

"No, Samuel, I can't stay."

His eyes opened wide. "What do you mean? Will I be all alone? I'm just a little boy." His bottom lip quivered.

"You will be four then, a big boy, big enough to live with Eli and learn. Until then I want you with me all the time."

The morning that Elkana left with Penina and her children, Samuel waved goodbye and turned to Chana: "Now the rest of the song!"

> The bows of the mighty are broken
> And the faltering are girded with strength.

> Men once sated must hire out for bread;
> Men once hungry hunger no more.

"I understand that, Ima. It means that God determines what happens to us and our lives can turn upside down in a flash."

> While the barren woman bears seven,
> The mother of many is forlorn.

"Will you have seven babies, Ima, and Penina lose her children?"

> The Lord deals death and gives life,
> Casts down into Sheol and raises up.
> The Lord makes poor and makes rich;
> He casts down, He also lifts high.
> He raises the poor from the dust,
> Lifts up the needy from the dunghill,
> Setting them with nobles,
> Granting them seats of honor.
> For the pillars of the earth are the Lord's,
> He has set the world upon them.
> He guards the steps of His faithful,
> But the wicked perish in darkness—
> For not by strength shall men prevail.

"Is that it?" Samuel asked when Chana paused for a long time. "No, it needs a conclusion. The words are in my brain, but I haven't organized them yet," she replied. "Let's work together on this long part." And the two recited and repeated it over and over until Samuel had memorized it.

Finally, on the day that they were expecting Elkana's return, Chana, standing next to her son at the window that overlooked the winding road leading to Shilo, told him: "I've completed it."

> The foes of the Lord shall be shattered;
> He will thunder against them in the heavens.
> The Lord will judge the ends of the earth.
> He will give power to His King,
> And triumph to His anointed one.

"Will we have a king, Ima? I don't want us to have a king."

"Why not, Samuel? All other nations have kings."

"We're not like others. You told me that only we have God, God is our king."

Musing over this, Chana thought to herself, "but the words that came to me were these words. It's as though the Lord put them into my head."

The following year, at age four, Samuel was weaned. He was a thoughtful serious boy, and he had accepted his destiny to remain with Eli in Shilo. The entire family made the pilgrimage, and, once there, Chana and Elkana took Samuel to the house of God to Eli.

Chana said, "Please, my lord: as you live, I am the woman who stood here beside you four years ago pleading with God. It was this boy I prayed for, and the Lord granted me what I asked of Him, and you had blessed me too. I, in turn, have vowed to lend him to God for as long as he lives."

Eli, taken aback, looked at Elkana, Chana and Samuel. He remembered the incident clearly, and remarked that the boy strongly resembled his mother. "Are you prepared to stay with me or not?" he asked Samuel.

"I am ready to stay," answered the boy in his high voice.

"Why will you stay?"

"To learn to read and write."

"Why?"

"To copy the Torah and to record great events, and…" Samuel stopped. Eli said: "Those are two noble reasons; do you have a third?"

Looking at his mother, Samuel added, "And to write my mother's poetry for all the people of Israel to read and chant to God."

"Excellent poetry is valued very highly," said Eli as he nodded to Chana and Elkana, taking Samuel's hand to lead him to his home. "Why don't you recite some of it to me as I show you to your room…"

"Be brave Chana," said Elkana. "You too," she whispered, talking his hand. "We will see him once a year as we come for the holiday."

"Yes, and I will make him clothing from year to year as he grows."

Before disappearing into the building, Eli turned back to the couple and addressed Elkana: "May the Lord grant you children by this woman in place of the loan that she made to the Lord." He turned back, Samuel waved, and they were gone.

"What are you thinking, Chana?"

With a grin she replied: "Wouldn't you like a girl next time?"

Notes

The Biblical texts for this chapter are in I Samuel and II Samuel. The translation of the poem is from the TANAKH published by the Jewish Publication Society, 1985.

For background material, I recommend Morris Silver, *Prophets and Markets: the Political Economy of Ancient Israel* (Kluwer Academic Publisher, 1982), chapters 5-10; Oded Borowski, *Daily Life in Biblical Times* (Society of Biblical Literature, 2003); E. W. Barber, *Women's Work: the First 20,000 Years. Women, Cloth, and Society in Early Times* (W. W. Norton, 1994); Jennie R. Ebeling, *Women's Lives in Biblical Times* (T & T Clark International, 2010), chapters 2, 4, 5, 6.

David's Wives:
Michal, Avigayil, Bathsheba

Merav and Michal were supervising the preparation of the evening meal, under the sharp-eyed overseer of all, their mother. They heard running footsteps outside the house and the harsh breathing of the approaching person. Into the room burst one of the young messengers whose job it was to bring news from King Saul, who was on the battlefield, to his family, living a few miles away.

"What happened? What happened?" the women fearfully asked, for it was unusual for the messenger to rush so. Michal held her breath, fearing that the Philistine giant had won the one-to-one combat and that her father had been taken prisoner or hurt.

Gulping down some water that someone had handed to him, the messenger took a deep breath and started his report:

"The giant, Goliath, came out as he has every day for weeks, challenging and taunting and cursing us. But today he was met in combat—but by a boy, a youth—who did not use armor, but a slingshot to bring him down! Then with Goliath's own sword this youth cut off the giant's head, holding it up for all to see. The Israelite army yelled as one man and charged down the hill at the Philistines. Victory is ours!"

He drank some more water, and then repeated his news, this time filling in as many details as he could. Concluding, he told the women that the king would be back that evening, and to prepare a festive meal for him, his sons, and the new hero, David.

Amidst the frenzy of preparation and excitement, Merav said to Michal: "I wonder what he looks like, this boy-hero."

"Why?" asked the younger sister, "do you think Father will finally agree to a match for you?"

"Why not? I'm sixteen already and that is more than old enough for marriage."

"Yes, but you are the king's daughter and Father only agrees to marriages that are good for him politically. You may end up being married to the son of a powerful tribal leader to ensure unity of Father's kingdom."

"The same holds true for you, Michal, so don't get any romantic ideas about anyone." Merav sighed. "I wish I were just like any other young woman and not a king's daughter."

"Nonsense. You love being important and having slaves and watching the goings-on in the house."

"I heard that other kings live in palaces, not just in a large house like this," said Merav, returning to her favorite topic. "If Father is King of Israel, why don't we live like other royalty?"

Michal replied in a bored voice, "Because Father is modest and is one of the people and he doesn't want to impose more taxes on the people to pay for useless luxury. We've talked this topic to death. Here, my job is done and the soups are ready. Mother is supervising the baking and your job is the fruit and vegetables. I'm going to fix this rotten hair of mine and put on a nicer robe."

She moved away from her sister and headed out of the hot kitchen area into the cooler corridor leading to the women's quarters. She glanced at the vines growing over the trellis in the center of the courtyard, nodding in approval that the wide leaves were providing a good amount of shade. She loved sitting in the arbor-like center smelling the sweet evening odors of the fruit trees outside the house. But she had no time for that at the moment, as she hurried to the room she shared with her older sister. The slavewoman who had taken care of the sisters since childhood, was in the small room that led into her room. As usual, she was weaving, this time a very thin wool fabric of a lovely shade of light blue.

"This will match your sister's blue eyes", said the older woman, "then I will make one in a rose shade for you, to complement your black eyes and hair."

"My hair!" groaned Michal. "I can't keep it in place. The curls just move this way and that no matter how hard I try to keep them straight!"

"Your hair is beautiful and you look just like your brother, Jonathan. Look at what a handsome man he is."

Michal replied, "Perhaps, but at least he can keep his hair short. I have the heavy hot mop with me all the time. I wish I were a man! Life is so much easier for men."

The older woman chuckled as she went to help Michal find another robe. "Much easier, like sitting out at the battlefield in the hot sun, not knowing if you are going to survive the day."

"I meant on a daily basis, not at a time of war."

"Israel has been at war for decades. That's how your father got me. Don't forget that I was one of the many prisoners taken when your father's army destroyed my town."

"Yes, yes. Let's change the topic. Here, help me with my hair. Just put it into one long braid down my back." As the slave helped Michal, Merav came rushing in.

"They're here! Father is back and I got a glimpse at the David. He's no boy! He's at least eighteen and he's gorgeous! Quick, help me into my dark blue robe. And I want the new long gold earrings."

The slave quickly finished Michal's hair, as she looked at her reflection in the small shiny brass mirror. The slave then moved to help Merav who had already dropped her work robe on the carpet. Michal left the room, curiosity leading her to the main eating area where all the noise was centered.

"Boo!" came a masculine voice behind her.

"Jonathan," she cried as she whirled around and hugged her brother, tears coming to her eyes. "I was so worried."

"It's over. Goliath is dead and Father is ecstatic. Come and meet David. He's a wonderful person, and so talented too. He plays music and composes poetry, and…"

"Jonathan," interrupted Michal, "I think you finally found a friend. I'm so happy for you, and…"

"Come," he repeated, grabbing her hand. Jonathan dragged her into the large room where their father was seated on a low bench atop a pile of pillows, leaning comfortably backwards against the wall. Seated on the carpeted floor to his left was a beardless young man with a head full of bright auburn hair. At their entrance, he turned to face Jonathan and as his face broke into a wide smile, Michal caught her breath.

"Well," King Saul stated, "you have finally come to welcome me home! Come here Michal and embrace your father." As she walked forward to kiss her father's hand, Saul added casually, "and this is David, slayer of Goliath, who will be staying with us for a while."

Michal nodded in his direction, and the full smile was now directed at her. "Brown eyes?" she thought, "or green? Or both?"

"Your father thinks that I can leave my flocks of sheep to fend for themselves," David said in a deep musical voice.

"No, I just think that since that army can now disperse, your brothers can return home to care for the sheep," answered King Saul.

"But how can they disperse, Sire? One victory is not enough. The Philistines have to be pushed back to the coastal area," said Jonathan. "And David can help."

Merav came bursting into the room just then.

"Father, welcome home," she said moving forward to kiss his hand.

"Is all this finery in my honor?" Saul asked teasingly looking at her robe and jewelry.

"Oh father," Merav pleaded, "don't embarrass me." She then turned to David and said, "Welcome to our household. My name is Merav."

David acknowledged her with his beaming smile, but before anything more could be said, the King's wife entered the room, leading the slaves who were carrying all of the food on various copper trays which were then placed on tripods in front of the king, David, Jonathan, and the other princes who came trooping in. The women, unlike in most households, sat at the farther end of the room and ate alongside the men. Conversation was sparse as everyone was hungry.

Later that night, as the sisters lay on their straw pallets, covered only with light woolen blankets, Merav confided that she thought she was in love.

"Don't do this to yourself," warned Michal talking as much to herself as to her sister. "We have no say in who we marry."

"I can dream, can't I?" responded Merav. "Did you see that smile? And how lean and strong he is…"

"But he is short compared to Father and Jonathan."

"And you," added Merav, "but he's just right for me."

David's Wives: Michal, Avigayil, Bathsheba

* * *

Three weeks passed and the relationship between King Saul and David gradually changed. Everyone in the household was upset because of this.

"Why is Father acting like this?" asked Merav. "He sits on this royal chair and watches David like a hawk. He wants him there to play the lyre and sing to him when his black moods hit, and then he stares as if with hatred when he's feeling fine."

"I have a feeling that this goes back to that time, many years ago, when Father and the prophet Samuel had that confrontation over the King of Amalek. Father never told us what happened, but he was never the same after that. And Samuel never came to see us again."

"I don't miss that angry old man. He scared me."

"Don't say that! He is God's messenger and I think that Father did something wrong then," mused Michal. "That's also when Father's black moods started. I imagine that everything is connected.

"I decided to talk to Father about my love for David," announced Merav. "I'll take my chances on what he will do."

That afternoon, Merav excitedly told her sister that Saul had reacted positively to her declaration. But Michal had her suspicions. "Tell me exactly what Father said."

"Father sat there for a few minutes and then got this funny look on his face. He mumbled something that sounded like "Let them get him." But that makes no sense. Well, I don't care what Father said, for he will talk to David tonight."

Michal, always practical, asked: "What will the brideswealth be? David is poor but proud, and you are the king's daughter."

"I hadn't thought of that! What if David says no? I'll die."

"You won't die. You'll marry someone else who can provide a huge brideswealth," responded her sister.

Michal's prediction proved true, for the negotiation over the brideswealth got bogged down, and Saul's undiplomatic way of talking upset David who was certainly interested in marrying Saul's daughter, although personally he preferred Michal who so much resembled her brother. Meanwhile, one of the most powerful of the Israelite tribal leaders pushed ahead with his own plans, and before Merav knew it, she was married off to his son.

"But father," she had cried, "you said that you would have me marry David! I love David!"

"Everyone loves David. The people love him more than me. They sing songs in his honor! Next thing he'll want my kingdom," Saul had replied. "You will marry Adriel, and that is it! The negotiations have been completed."

After Merav moved to her new home, Michal, feeling lonely, climbed her favorite olive tree as she had as a child. Jonathan found her there.

"I thought you would be here, in your old haunt."

"Jonathan, I miss Merav and I don't like growing up. She did not want to marry Adriel. Why can't we choose who we want?"

"That's the way it has always been. I didn't choose my wife either—Father did. I'm not saying that I don't like her, for I do. But David talks of love, passionate love. I wonder if any of us will ever feel it."

"I feel it," whispered Michal.

"What?" said her brother.

"I fell great love, but it's a secret."

Jonathan looked at her straight in the eyes and softly said: "You love him, don't you? Well, if it will make you feel any better, David always preferred you over Merav. " Seeing her eyes light up, he mused, "how can we handle Father and David at the same time? I don't trust Father when it comes to David, but I think I know how to do this. Trust me, Michal. My plan will work because it's roundabout."

One of Jonathan's trusted men, while in the private presence of the king, told him quietly that he had heard a rumor that Michal was in love with David. The king liked the idea and told his man to tell David privately that the king would agree to the match. When David told this third party that he was a poor man and could not pay brideswealth for a princess, Saul sent the message that for a hero, a heroic act served just as well as monetary or physical brideswealth. What kind of heroic act? The king would be happy with one hundred foreskins of the Philistines. Saul's warped mind imagined and hoped that David would be killed before accomplishing this. David on the other hand, happily accepted these conditions and proceeded with his men to kill two hundred Philistines. Defeated in his plan, Saul had to proceed with the marriage.

An ecstatically happy bride was led from the women's quarters into the public room of the king's house. Michal couldn't believe that this was really happening and that David was to be hers. There he was, dressed in a beautiful robe, his hair like burnished copper, his eyes looking into hers, two beacons of light shining through her gossamer veil. The musicians played, and Saul took her hand, placing it on David's. As her veil was lifted, David's happy smile filled Michal with joy, and the young couple almost danced as they left the gathering in the direction of their small accommodation, attached to the royal house but lower down on the hill. The only shadow cast was the look on Saul's face as Michal turned to smile at him; it was a look of naked fear and hate as he stared at David.

Not long after their marriage, David came stomping into the house.

"Your father did it again," he fumed. "He tried to kill me again! How many times can I evade his spear before my luck runs out? This time your brother was a witness, as the spear missed me and stuck in the wall."

"David, beloved, I would do anything to help you. Let me go to my father's house and listen to the gossip in the women's quarters. I will be able to judge if it's merely a black episode or if my father is really out to kill you."

"Go, my Michal. I hope it's merely an episode, for your sake as well as mine, for if he is intent on killing me, I will have to flee to the mountains."

Michal hurried up the hill to the royal house, returning home as the sun set. Almost at her heels, a group of King Saul's personal guard marched down and stationed themselves in front of David's house. For Michal this was the culminating factor.

"David, if you do not flee for your life tonight, my father will have you killed first thing in the morning. Don't argue with me, and move quickly, beloved, for the king's guards are in front of the house." She led him to the rear of their house where the hill dropped precipitously. Tying together thick cloth and lengths of rope, the two formed a rope long enough to reach from the window to the hillside. Hugging each other tearfully, Michal pushed David ahead, and holding the upper end of the rope, she watched him slowly disappear out of the window. When she felt his weight gone, she rushed over to the window in time to catch a brief wave before he disappeared into the dark shadows of the night.

Turning back to the house, Michal rushed over to the corner of the main room, grabbed the *terafim*, or good luck figure, that David had teased her about, saying that those old things were old-wives' tales and did not belong in Israelite houses. "Well," she thought, "let's hope it will bring good luck tonight." Lugging the large wooden figure, she put it on David's bed and covered it with a colorfully woven blanket. On second thought, she grabbed in inflatable goatskin water holder and put it where his head would be, pulling the blanket up higher.

Just then there was a banging at the front door, Michal walked slowly to the door, forcing herself to breathe normally.

"Who knocks so at this hour?"

"The king's guard. Open up so that we may accompany David into the king's presence!"

Michal opened the door but blocked entry. She knew that her height prevented a close look at the bed, and she also knew that the guards could see the outline on the bed. "My husband is ill and cannot accompany you. Tell that to my father the king." The guards hesitated, then left, but before she had a chance to do anything more, they returned.

"The king orders us to bring David into his presence in his bed!" They pushed past Michal and immediately recognized that the shape on the bed was not a man's. Pulling the cover off and seeing the *terafim*, the leader of the guards turned to Michal and said almost sadly: "I think you had better come with us."

The storyteller stopped talking. His audience—the master of the house, his wives, their children, and all their slaves—seated around the visitor collectively held their breath. The storyteller raised his goblet slowly to his mouth to enjoy the flavor of the new wine to its fullest, when a child of about six spoke for all:

"So what happened next?"

The storyteller finished swallowing, turned to the child and smiling under his thick beard, responded:

"Next? It's very late. See, the moon is in the midst of the sky and everyone has to arise with the sun to put in a full day's work. If my host wishes, I can put off my departure and continue my tale tomorrow evening after we eat."

Everyone turned to the patriarch who genially smiled and tousled the head of the questioning child who was sitting close to his grand father.

"Certainly you should extend your stay with us. We are all interested in the stories of our favorite king, King David. Life was so exciting then."

"Yes. Nowadays under King Solomon life seems to be more humdrum. But, " he hastened to add, "safer."

"Yes, safer. But safe can be boring… To bed, everyone. Our visitor will continue his tale tomorrow night."

* * *

When Michal was brought before her father, King Saul, she knew that her life was on the line. Her father was raging like an insane man. Never had the black mood been so bad. What could she do? To tell Saul that her love of David came first and so she had saved him might lead her father to slay her. To tell Saul that she put him first both as her father and as her king would be a lie but would save her momentarily. Surely a white lie could not have bad consequences.

"Why did you play that trick on me and let my enemy escape safely?" roared Saul, hold his sword out at his daughter.

"Because," answered a shaking Michal, "he said to me: "Help me or I will slay you."

"A little lie," she thought, "how much harm could it do?"

Saul lowered the sword.

"So he forced you to help. He left you behind. He deserted you…"

Michal did not like the look in Saul's eyes, but at least the black mood was dissipating. "A little lie," she thought again, "how much harm can it do?"

The Biblical Woman

* * *

"Did it do any harm? Did it?" pressed the verbal child.

"Give him a chance. Let him tell his tale his own way," responded his father.

"If you can't keep quiet, you will go to your bed," warned his mother. "Shh, now."

Everyone settled down on their pillows. The narrator sipped from his wine cup.

"How much harm from a little white lie? It only destroyed Michal's life."

"Not David's?" queried the patriarch.

"Shh," said his grandson.

Everyone chuckled and the storyteller began again.

* * *

When David realized that he could not return home for fear of his life, he met his beloved friend Prince Jonathan in the fields where they bade each other an emotional farewell. Little did David know that he would never see Jonathan again.

He fled to the Judean hills and gradually gathered around him a ragtag army of runaway slaves, deserting soldiers, and landless peasants. He was able to whip them into a sold group unified in their love and admiration for him. They traveled, some six hundred men, from place to place in Israel and earned their food by doing service to local landowners and owners of large flocks of sheep and goats.

There was a man in Maon whose possessions were in Carmel. The man was very wealthy; he owned three thousand sheep and a thousand goats. His name was Naval and his wife's name was Avigayil. She was intelligent and beautiful, but the man, although of the noble family of Caleb ben Yefuneh, was a hard man, an evil man.

At the time of the sheep shearing, which is a time of thanksgiving for the survival of the animals and the provision of wool for garments and blankets and trade, David was in the wilderness near Carmel. He dispatched ten young men, instructing them:

"Go up to Carmel and when you come to Naval, greet him in my name and say: "To life! Greetings to you and yours! I hear that you are shearing. As you know, your shepherds have been with us in the wilderness and we protected them from all loss. Ask your men and they will tell you. So please receive my young men graciously, for we have come on a festive occasion. Please give your servants and your servant David whatever you can."

David's young men memorized this message, understanding that it was a polite upper class way of asking for payment. But when they delivered this message to Naval, he responded:

"Who is David? Who is the son of Jesse?" Sneeringly he went on so that all could hear. "There are many slaves nowadays who run away from their masters. Should I then take my bread and my water and the meat that I slaughtered for my own shearers and give them to men who come from I don't know where?"

Naval turned his back on David's men, as his own men murmured among themselves. Thereupon David's men retraced their steps and when they got back, they told him what Naval had said. David flew into a fury and ordered his men:

"Gird your swords!"

He stomped over to his belongings and pulled out a large sword which he girded while directing some four hundred of his ablest men to fall into place. As they strode out, the two hundred young, lame, and old men remained behind to guard the baggage.

* * *

"Oh yes, a battle. David will slice Naval's head off, just like he did to Goliath!" one of the boys shouted in glee.

"Hold your tongue! You don't know what will happen," said an older brother.

"Does the beautiful Avigayil do anything?" asked a sister, softly but clearly. "I do like it when women do things too."

"Women don't do anything but have babies," stated a ten-year-old brother.

"Nonsense," replied one of the women. "You forget Deborah. And Miriam, and..."

The storyteller intervened: "Yes Avigayil is important here. Remember. I described her first as intelligent and then as beautiful. That was not an accident." His voice then returned to storyteller sing-song mode.

* * *

One of Naval's young men sneaked out of the shearing area and rushed as fast as he could to report the incident to Avigayil. Panting, he gasped the story out, adding:

"But the men were truly very friendly to us and protected us while we were outside. They were a wall about us by night and by day while we tended the flocks! Please do something, for from what I heard about David, he will not forgive Naval but will harm him and all of us. No one can approach your husband for he is so very nasty!"

Avigayil quickly ordered her slaves to gather two hundred flat breads. Others she sent rushing for two jars of wine; still others fetched five already roasted sheep, and five measures of dried grain.

"Let me see, let me take some more luxurious things as well. Go fetch one hundred cakes of dried raisins, and two hundred cakes of pressed figs! Quickly. There's no time to lose!"

People rushed back and forth as Avigayil directed the loading of the food on the pack asses. She directed her young man to ride on ahead, as her slave brought her the large elegant gray ass that was Avigayil's pride and joy. The saddle and reins were made of the best leather and decorated with red stones. She mounted the ass which brayed with excitement, and with firm kicks from both feet in his sides, the animal moved quickly in the direction of David's camp.

A half hour passed, and Avigayil's ass started climbing the narrow road leading around and up the mountain where the slave had told her that David was to be found. The drop was steep to her right, but Avigayil was a practiced rider and knew no fear. She was concentrating both on her riding and on the tactics she would use with David. Her knowledge of him was only secondhand, but what she had heard had impressed her. She particularly liked his poetry, which had been spread by word of mouth.

David, meanwhile, was marching purposefully down the mountainside, following the same path as Avigayil was climbing. He loudly stated to his men that he was planning to wipe out all of Naval's household for the insult that he had given him. "He has paid me evil for good!"

Just then David came face to face with Avigayil. She realized immediately who he was because his copper-colored hair and beard were famous. She had to stop him, and she used the tactic of surprise well. She quickly dismounted from the ass and threw herself face down, bowing to the ground. David was speechless at the sight of an obviously upper class woman acting this way, and on a mountain road yet. Prostrate at his feet, she pleaded;

"Let the blame be mine, my lord, but let your servant speak to you. Please hear my plea! Please pay no attention to that wretched man, Naval, for he is what his name says—he is a boor, or worse, a stinking piece of dead carrion."

Seeing that she had his complete attention, Avigayil arose. She knew that she had to state her case clearly and succinctly. "Your servant did not see the young men sent by you. I would have dealt differently with them than did Naval, and praise the Lord who has kept you from seeking vengeance and getting blood on your hands. Here!" Avigayil leaped from the first idea to the next, and dramatically gesturing to the laden asses which had just reached the curve of the mountain path.

"Here is the present which your servant has brought to you, my lord. Please, let all the food be divided among your young men." She noted that the eyes of David's men had widened as they noted the roast meat, the raisins, the figs, and the bread; they guessed that the large jugs contained wine. David too noted this, but he kept his eyes on Avigayil. Emboldened, she continued: "Please pardon my boldness. May the Lord grant my lord an enduring house, because my lord is fighting the battles of the Lord, and no wrong has been found in you."

David was paying close attention and appreciating the play on words of Avigayil's statements. Flushing at his obvious appreciation, Avigayil decided that here was a person to really appreciate her verbal abilities, so she carefully crafted her next statements playing on David's poetry as well as his military prowess.

"If anyone sets out to pursue you and seek your life, the life of my lord will be bound up in the bundle of life in the care of the Lord, and God will fling away the lives of your enemies as from the hollow of a sling."

Nodding his enjoyment, David silently awaited the climax of her speech, which he recognized as approaching from the timbre of her voice.

"And when the Lord has accomplished the promise of appointing you ruler over Israel," continued Avigayil boldly, voicing what most Israelites knew would happen, "do not let this incident with Naval be a cause for stumbling or bad reputation, that you have shed blood needlessly and that you sought vengeance with your own hands."

The full impact of her statement registered with David, who absorbed it to the core of his soul and recognized its validity. Thinking that her presentation was over, David opened his mouth to respond, when Avigayil, in a low voice that only he could hear, added, her cheeks bright red: "And when the Lord has prospered my lord, remember your servant."

David responded to Avigayil so that all the men could hear:

"Praise the Lord who sent you to me this day! Blessed be your prudence, and blessed be you for restraining me from seeking blood vengeance by my own hands. Had this not happened I surely would have destroyed all that was Naval's." He motioned to his men to accept Avigayil's gift of food, and as the men moved here and there, David looked straight into her eyes and said softly, "Go home safely. See I have heeded your plea, and" with a wide grin, "respected your wish."

Waving goodbye, Avigayil remounted her grey ass and headed down the mountainside, analyzing her actions, her words, and her unusual boldness with David. Then her mind turned to more pressing issues: how was she to tell Naval how close he had come to death. When she arrived home, she found him feasting and drinking one cup of wine after another. She decided therefore that she would wait until morning, and retired to her bedroom. Late the next morning, she found Naval in the public part of the house where he was just rising from where he had slept in a drunken stupor.

"Oh, my head. Get me something." He ordered his wife. She brought him orange juice and water to wash with. The slave brought in fresh bread and fruit, but Naval waved her away.

"Naval, can you hear me?" asked Avigayil.

"How could anyone not hear you? Your bell-like voice goes through the core of my brain this morning. Say what you have to say without speeches, please. I have no head for you this morning."

Tersely Avigayil told Naval everything, and upon realizing how close he had come to death, Naval had a stroke. He became like a stone. Avigayil had him cared for, but after ten days Naval died, and Avigayil mourned him for seven days and then for thirty, as was required of a wife. In her head she thanked the Lord for setting her free.

Up in the mountains word came to David of Naval's death, and he praised the Lord for punishing Naval without his doing wrong. He calculated the thirty days and sent messengers to propose marriage to Avigayil. As a rich widow, Avigayil was her own person who did not have to rely on an older relative to arrange a marriage. The same held true for David. There was no question of brideswealth. Avigayil knew that she would be the wife of the future king. She also knew, wise as she was, that she would have to share him, for he was sure to marry other women. Weighing and balancing the issues, Avigayil decided to follow her heart, for David pleased her immensely. So she rose quickly, mounted her prized ass, and with five of her slaves, followed David's messengers. The living quarters were primitive, and the marriage was without the great celebration that had accompanied her first nuptials. Avigayil could not have cared less.

* * *

"But what about Michal?" asked one of the girls. "You left her without David. Didn't she still love him?"

"Yes, she loved him," responded the storyteller, "but because of her lie, Saul saw David's desertion as the first half of a divorce. In accepting this, Saul completed the divorce, and gave her in marriage to Palti ben Laish."

"But she didn't love him," protested one child.

"But David didn't divorce her!" protested a second.

"Correct on both counts, and those are the ingredients of tragedy. The hour grows late. My voice is giving out."

Again all eyes went to the patriarch.

"Yes, yes. He will stay over and continue tomorrow evening. To bed one and all."

* * *

The sad day arrived when Saul and Jonathan were killed in battle. David mourned and composed his famous dirge for them. Soon after, he moved to Hebron where the men of Judah anointed David king. But there was still a party, led by General Abner, that backed a younger son of Saul, anointing him. The war between the two lasted almost two years, with David's supporters gaining in strength. Abner, for personal reasons, decided to join the winning side and sent a message to David of his desire. David agreed to make a pact on one condition:

"Do not appear before me unless you bring with you Michal the daughter of Saul."

At the same time, David sent messengers to Saul's son demanding:

"Give me my wife Michal for whom I paid a brideswealth of an act of courage."

* * *

"So David did love her!" sighed one of the teenage daughters.

"Silly," responded her brother. "He sent for her for political reasons. David was so clever."

"How does politics come into marriage?" asked another.

"Michal was Saul's daughter. This was a civil war. By showing that he was married to Saul's daughter, David was making his rule more legitimate," responded the wise brother.

"But wasn't she married to Paltiel? David can't remarry a wife who was married to someone else," stated one of the patriarch's wives.

"But David never divorced her. Only Saul saw David's departure as an act of divorce. It was her marriage to Paltiel that was not proper," another wife said.

"Yet if they lived together—Michal and Paltiel—David can't take her back!"

"What a mess!" stated one of the younger children.

Amidst the chuckles, the attention refocused on the storyteller, who had been enjoying the discussion.

"You are all right, and yes, it was a mess. Michal still loved David, but David only wanted her back for political reasons. Michal came and found that not only did she have to share David with six other wives, but that because of her unclear legal status, David had difficulty deciding if he should co-habit with her. There she was, in the large house in Hebron, absolutely miserable.

* * *

The civil war ended with the death of Saul's son. David then felt strong enough to take Jerusalem, and in so doing, ordered the Ark of the Lord to be brought into Jerusalem. The day that it arrived was a day of great rejoicing, and David, dressed in a simple tunic, leaped and whirled in religious ecstasy before the Lord, he blessed the people, and distributed huge amounts of breads and cakes to them. David then went to his palace and to his family still feeling uplifted and joyous, only to be met by Michal, her voice full of disdain:

"Didn't the king of Israel do himself honor today, exposing himself today in the sight of the slave girls, as one of the riffraff might do!"

David looked hard at the woman who had been the wife of his youth. He saw her bitterness and anger and made his decision. "It was before the Lord who chose me over your father and appointed me ruler over the people of Israel that I danced, and will continue to do so even if you think it dishonorable, you who are the only one to think so."

David turned his back on her, but did not send her away. She lived out her life in the palace, a victim of circumstances.

* * *

"That's not fair," sniffled one of the girls.

"Life isn't fair all the time," added another.

"Did David ever fall in love?" asked a third.

"Love! Why do women always think of love?" said a curly haired boy of about twelve.

"Because it's important!"

"Is not."

"Is so."

"Yes, it can be important," slowly responded the storyteller. "And when David fell in love, it was with the wrong woman. But that is a tale unto itself…"

The patriarch looked at the storyteller. "I am beginning to think that you should move in here."

"Well, I usually do stay for a few weeks with a host before moving on to the next town or to the next household. This way, many parts of Israel can learn of the stories of our kings."

"Yes, that does make sense. I know that all of us sitting here are memorizing your stories. All right, everyone, to bed. Tomorrow night we will hear of David's forbidden love."

* * *

At the turn of the year, in the springtime, David sent his army out to battle Israel's enemy Ammon, but he stayed in Jerusalem. Late in the afternoon, after his nap, David walked along the flat roof-balcony of his palace from where he could survey the entire city. He saw a movement below, and on the rooftop of a nearby large house he saw a woman bathing. She seemed oblivious to any possible onlooker, possibly because the only edifice higher than hers was the palace, and David was usually out with his men during battle season. She immersed herself in a rooftop ritual bath, utilizing the stored rainwater.

The woman was very beautiful, and David was overcome. He immediately sent a servant to find out who the woman who lived in that house was, for even though the buildings were close to each other, women's and men's lives tended to be separate, so he did not recognize her. The servant reported back:

"She is Bathsheba, daughter of Eliam, and wife of Uriah the Hittite."

"She's married!" thought David. "Of course she's married. She's too beautiful not to be married. And to my officer Uriah. I even like Uriah."

He fumed and fretted, and barely ate supper. All he could think about was white skin and long auburn hair. At midnight he could stand it no longer and he sent messengers to fetch her. "If she comes, that is my destiny; if she does not, that too is my destiny," he thought feverishly. She came and David led her into his private chamber, dismissing all the servants but one. There was no conversation, just two adults united in their sin. Before dawn, the lone trusted servant escorted her through the palace and back to her home.

David busied himself for the next two weeks, studiously avoiding the rooftop view of the city. He took care of a backlog of bureaucratic matters, tended to the multiple duties of kingship, and sent and received messengers from the front line of battle. Four weeks passed and a messenger brought David a private word for his ears only.

"I am with child."

David knew that it was from Bathsheba and he immediately set about covering up their deed. He sent a message to his general to send Uriah back to David to personally report on the battle. Uriah arrived, dusty and sweaty, marching into the palace to present his news. David listened carefully, nodding from time to time. Then he said:

"Uriah, go down to your house, bathe yourself and eat."

Uriah bowed to his monarch and left the audience chamber, but did not return home. Instead Uriah slept at the entrance of the palace, where the officers on duty had their quarters. When one of the servants reported on this to David, the king sent again for Uriah.

"You just came from a dusty hot journey; why did you not go to your house?"

Uriah bowed to David, and with his honest open face replied: "The ark of the Lord and all the Judean army are living out in the open. How can I go home and eat and drink and sleep with my wife—I cannot in good conscience do this!"

David thought quickly, for it was exactly this last item that interested him. Only thus could the pregnancy be attributed to Uriah.

"Stay in Jerusalem today, and tomorrow I will send you off."

So Uriah stayed and was invited to dine at the king's table. David managed to get Uriah quite drunk, hoping that the wine would induce him to return to his wife. But Uriah slept with the officers again.

Defeated by Uriah's honesty and conscientiousness, David sat down to write a letter himself to his general. In it he ordered the general to place Uriah in the thick of the fighting, then to draw back so that he could be killed. Uriah himself carried these secret sealed orders back to the front, and sure enough, brave Uriah was killed. The report of the battle and the deaths was carried by fast messenger to David.

When Uriah's wife heard that her husband was dead, she lamented over her husband of whom she was very fond. After the period of mourning was over, David sent and had her brought to the palace where he married her and she bore him a son.

*　*　*

"Wait, storyteller. You go too quickly. You give no details. You seem to want to rush through this," one of the women stopped the teller of the tale.

"Yes, you seem to dislike this story."

"I just realized—David couldn't marry her after the mourning period. A widow cannot remarry for ninety days," put in the patriarch himself.

"But father, they couldn't wait three month for she was pregnant."

"Pregnant by David, not by Uriah."

"David was an adulterer."

"Worse, by setting up Uriah, he was a murderer."

"This is terrible."

"Did he get away with all of this?"

"I don't like this story."

The storyteller took a long drink of wine. He slowly looked around at the assembled extended family. Shaking his head sadly, he said: "Even great people are human, and the Lord seems to test us in our weaknesses. David's weakness was women. Or this one woman…" He sighed, and turning to his questioners, continued.

* * *

But the Lord was displeased with what David had done, and sent Nathan the prophet to the palace. Nathan was announced to the King who looked up in anticipation. He motioned the prophet forward with a broad smile of welcome. Without any of the niceties of state protocol, Nathan began to speak in his gruff, blunt way.

"There were two men in the same city, one rich and one poor. The rich man had many flocks but the poor man had only one ewe lamb that he tended and raised as a pet. One day a traveler came to the rich man, but he was such a miser, he would not kill an animal from his own flock to feed the guest, but he took the poor man's lamb and prepared it for the meal."

David flew into a rage against the man, for David's heart was soft and he hated injustice. "As the Lord lives, the man who did this deserves to die! He shall pay for the lamb four times over because he showed no pity."

Nathan was counting on David's reaction to the story, and rose to his full height, pointing an accusing finger at the king, who sat back in astonishment.

"You are that man! Thus says the Lord: "I anointed you King of Israel and I rescued you from Saul. I gave you his house and the house of Israel and Judah, and if that were not enough I would have given you twice more! Why then have you flouted the Lord's laws and done what displeases the Lord? You have had Uriah slain and you took his wife as your own. Therefore," thundered Nathan, "the sword will never depart from this house—because of your deeds. Your own house will rise against you and another man will sleep with your wives as an act of kingship. You acted in secret, but the Lord will make this happen in broad daylight!"

David's emotional reaction was swift.

"I stand guilty!" he confessed to all, penitent tears in his eyes.

Nathan replied in a calmer voice: "The Lord has remitted your sin; you shall not die. But your newborn shall. And three others too, for you gave judgment on a four-fold payment."

Nathan turned his back on a weeping contrite David, slowly walked out of the throne room, and returned home.

* * *

"How terrible," whispered a child.

"He deserved it."

"But the child did not."

"The child was a *mamzer*, born of a forbidden union. The whole world knew it now, and he would have been treated horribly."

"But he was a baby!"

"Did he die?" asked another child.

"Yes, he did, although David fasted and prayed in an attempt to save him," responded the storyteller.

"I don't like this story," said one of the young women.

"Wait," interrupted the tale teller. "Something unusual then happened."

"What?" they all asked in one voice.

"Bathsheba, who had suffered the loss of one baby, soon became pregnant again, and..." he paused.

"And?" they all breathed.

"They named him Solomon."

"Solomon? Our king? His mother is Bathsheba?"

"Yes. The Lord blessed this union and even Nathan came to bless him and give him the corresponding name "Yedidya."

"The Lord's ways are inscrutable!" intoned the patriarch.

"Did David lose three other sons?" asked one bright youngster.

"Yes, he lost Amnon, who was killed by Absalom, his half-brother. Then Absalom was killed for rebelling against David. The fourth son, Adoniyahu, was killed for treason as well, but only after David had died." The storyteller ticked off the list easily.

"I want to know about Bathsheba," interrupted an older wife. "If her son ruled..."

"Wait," interrupted the storyteller. "It almost didn't happen. Let me continue."

David's Wives: Michal, Avigayil, Bathsheba

* * *

King David grew old. He was only seventy when he died, but during his last years his body became very frail. He lost interest in ruling and withdrew into the privacy of his own quarters, only performing the absolute minimum of his duties. He even avoided his constantly bickering wives and children, and was cared for by an outsider, a young woman name Avishag, who had no political nor personal interest in the monarchy.

His son, the handsome Adoniyahu, next in line for the kingship according to age, simply could not wait for David to die to put forward his claim to the throne. In his impatience, he gathered around him a political-military group of loyalists and made a feast in which to declare his kingship. His main rival, his half-brother Solomon, and Solomon's supporters were not invited to the feast.

As soon as Nathan the Prophet, one of Solomon's main backers, learned of Adoniyahu's activities, he rushed to Bathsheba. He knew that he could not influence David alone, and he also knew that as *Gevira*, or mother of the Crown Prince, Bathsheba had open access to the king. There was no assurance that David would consent to even see Nathan, but Bathsheba could just walk into David's chambers and the guards would not stop her.

"You must have heard that Adoniyahu has claimed the kingship," Nathan declared to Bathsheba. At her nod, Nathan continued. "King David is ignorant of this deed, so you must act quickly so that you may save your life as well as that of your son Solomon. Go immediately to King David and say to him, reminding him, "Did you not swear to me, oh lord king, that our son Solomon will succeed you as king and sit on your throne?" When David agrees that he said that, continue with "Then why has Adoniyahu become king?" As you are saying this I will enter and confirm your words. Between the two of us, let us hope we can push David into action."

Bathsheba realized the wisdom of Nathan's advice, for surely Adoniyahu would slay Solomon, his main rival for the throne. So she dressed carefully, and with great trepidation that she did not show outwardly, Bathsheba entered David's chambers. She was momentarily distracted by how old and depressed David looked, and she had a fleeting memory of how vibrant he had been when they had first married. She shook off these memories while bowing before him. David, in a grumpy disinterested voice asked, "And what do you want?"

Knowing instinctively that David had no use for niceties, she got straight to the point. "My lord, you yourself swore to me by the Lord: "Your son Solomon shall succeed me as king and sit on my throne." At David's impatient nod of agreement, Bathsheba continued. "Yet now Adoniyahu has become king!" David looked startled. "See, even you the king know nothing of it. Yes, he has made a great feast for his followers to celebrate his kingship." David's attention was waning, so she continued quickly and with emphasis:

"The eyes of all Israel are on you, O lord king, to tell them officially who shall succeed you! I know it is hard to do, but otherwise when you lie with your fathers, my son Solomon and I will be regarded as traitors and killed."

Before David had a chance to dismiss her with an excuse that she was exaggerating, Nathan was announced by the guards. With David's permission, Nathan entered and bowing low, used his powerful bass voice to get the king's total attention.

"O lord king, you must have ordered that Adoniyahu should succeed you, for how else could he be celebrating his succession?" Nathan was wisely indirectly pointing out that Adoniyah's actions were treasonous; David had to come to that conclusion himself. "But why have you not informed me of this?"

David's anger at his son fired him finally into action. "Bathsheba!" he ordered. She stepped closed in anticipation. "As the Lord lives, the oath I swore to you the Solomon shall succeed me as king I will fulfill this very day!" She bowed low in homage to her husband the king, thus hiding from him her triumphant face.

"May my lord King David live forever!" she declared.

David summoned his chief priest and his leading general to join Nathan. "Take my loyal soldiers, put Solomon on my mule, bring him down to the Valley of Gihon where all of Israel can view the action, and anoint him king. Sound the shofar and shout "Long live King Solomon!" Then march up after him into the throne room where he will ascend the throne!"

As the three men rushed out of the chamber, Bathsheba watched David as his momentary burst of energy evaporated. The fire in his eyes slowly extinguished, and her heart went out to him. She helped Avishag raise him from his chair and put him into his bed. The two women looked at each other with the knowledge that David's end was near. With a sigh, Bathsheba leaned over and kissed her husband's forehead in a farewell gesture. She had succeeded in her goal: her son would be king within the hour. The king is dead, long live the king.

Notes

The Biblical texts for this chapter are I Samuel 17, 18, 19, 25. II Samuel 6, 11, 12, and I Kings 1.

For background material, I recommend James M. Miller and John H. Hayes, *A History of Ancient Israel and Judah* (Westminster John Knox Press, 2006); William H. Stiebing, *Ancient Near Eastern History and Culture* (Routledge, 2016); Jennie R. Ebeling, *Women's Lives in Biblical Times* (T & T Clark International, 2010), especially chapter 4.

Esther

The scribe sat at his low table looking over the many scraps of parchment before him. He had organized the hastily written notes into a more or less chronological sequence of events. Then, placing a new folio of parchment in front of him, he proceeded to prepare half a dozen quills for writing, trimming them to his precise needs. The ink was already in its decorated ceramic container to the right of his writing space.

The scribe had just been promoted out of the rank of copyists, and his assignment was so important that he broke into a sweat just thinking about what could happen should he not succeed. He forced himself to concentrate on what he was about to write. The chief scribe had chosen him in part because his writing was so beautiful and in part because the older man had recognized his intelligence and creativity. This was his chance. But how did one chronicle events that were at the same time clear and shadowy, straightforward yet contradictory? How much to include? How much and what to glide over?

He dipped the first quill into the black ink, and after a moment's hesitation, began to write: *It happened in the days of Ahashverosh, the Ahashverosh who reigned over a hundred and twenty seven provinces from India to Cush.* He dipped again, but, sensing someone looking over his shoulder, turned his head. The chief scribe was there.

"Good opening sentence," he complimented. "Remember, the queen wants as little as possible written about her. Write as much as you want about the king, about Haman, about her uncle Mordechai."

"Yes sir, I remember what you told me, but I do not understand."

"It is not for you to understand. Just do as she ordered."

"Yes sir, but..."

"No buts. If you have any doubts of how to word the sections on the queen, write them on scrap parchment and let me see them before they go into the scroll itself."

"Yes sir."

The older man nodded in satisfaction, leaving the small room to check up on all of the copyists who were down the hall in the large scriptorium of the palace. The young scribe took a deep breath, and, returning to his parchment, dipped the pen once more into the ink and wrote the next sentence: *In those days, when King Ahashverosh occupied the royal throne in the fortified city of Shushan...* He worked carefully all morning, and when the chief scribe next entered his room, the page was full and the first chapter completed. He handed the drying parchment to the chief scribe who read it over carefully. Looking up, he smiled broadly.

"I knew I made a good choice in promoting you. This is better than good. It is excellent. His Majesty will be most pleased. But the next part brings you to the queen. Be careful."

* * *

Some time later, when the anger of King Ahashverosh subsided, he thought of Vashti and what she had done and what had been decreed against her. The king's attendants said, "Let beautiful young women be sought for Your Majesty"... The scribe described the search for the new queen to replace the rebellious Queen Vashti, whose actions could have led to the rebellion of all women against their husbands. The king would choose the new queen himself. Now, how to introduce Esther. He left a space between the last word and the next sentence, indicating a new subject but one connected to the previous one.

In the capital city of Shushan lived a Jew named Mordechai, son of Ya'ir, son of Shim'i, son of Kish, a Benjaminite. He was of the first exile from Jerusalem and was foster father to his relative Hadassah, known too as Esther, who had lost both parents. *The young woman was shapely and beautiful, and when her father and mother died, Mordechai adopted her as his own daughter.*

The chief scribe materialized, startling his protégé with his comments: "Good, use as few words as possible. The queen's royal blood is subtly referred to this way."

"But what do I do now, sir? Do I openly write that she did not want to come to the palace? Do I write that the king cohabited with each young woman to sort of try them out?"

"Don't be ridiculous! The king has the right to do as he pleases. We can't question these things."

"And as a Jew—we all know about their peculiar eating habits and even more peculiar actions connected with their Sabbath—what do I write of Esther's long stay in the harem?"

"Nothing. Absolutely nothing! I told you of the queen's orders. Be creative. Think it through. I trust you to solve the problem of saying just enough but not too much." He left the younger man who did not write anything more that day. He had nightmares that night and awoke before dawn, to pace back and forth until his wife arose, to return shortly with a hot drink sweetened with honey. She smiled at him encouragingly. He dressed, ate a quick meal, and left for the palace arriving well before any of the other scribes. He had the oil lamps lit by the attending slave, and seated himself before his writing table where the partially written parchment awaited him. He dipped a fresh quill in the black ink and wrote.

When the king's order and edict was proclaimed, and when many young women were assembled in the capital of Shushan under the supervision of Hegai, Esther too was taken into the king's palace....The young woman pleased him and won his favor, and he hastened to furnish her with her cosmetics and her rations, as well as with the seven slaves who were her due from the King's palace; and he treated her and her slaves with special kindness in the harem. Esther did not reveal her people nor her birth, for Mordechai had told her not to reveal it. Every single day Mordechai would walk about in front of the courtyard of the harem, to learn how Esther was faring and what was happening to her.

The scribe sat back and reread the paragraph. "There," he thought. "By using the grammatical form *and she was taken* I've solved the problem. The subtle reader will understand, and the simple listener will just grasp the surface meaning. And by using my interview with Hegai this way, I've subtly made him an active party in helping meet Esther's personal needs."

The palace was buzzing with activity, and the chief scribe glanced in the room. Noting the lit oil lamps, he said: "I see you arrived very early. Did you write anything more?"

"One brief section, sir."

He moved out of the way, blowing out the lamps as his supervisor read and reread the paragraph. Nodding finally, he said: "Subtle, very subtle. And you have also introduced the secret of her religion. Go on, go on." He put the parchment back on the low writing table, ordering one of the slaves to go fetch some fresh pomegranate juice for the scribe. With a grin, he left saying: "You need energy. Order anything you want, except wine—that will put you to sleep. You must stay sharp. Very sharp."

The scribe easily described the repetitive experience of each young woman's night with the king and subsequent move to the concubines' harem in three sentences. But he was stuck when it came to describing why Esther's arrival before the king differed from all of her predecessors. He could not go before the king and ask questions. In the end he opted for simple declarative statements.

When the turn came for Esther, daughter of Avihayil—niece of Mordechai, who had adopted her as his daughter—to go to the king, she did not ask for anything but what Hegai, the king's eunuch, guardian of the women, advised. Esther won the admiration of all who saw her. Esther was taken to King Ahashverosh, to his royal palace, on the tenth of the month of Tevet, in the seventh year of his reign. The king loved Esther more than all the women, and she won his favor more than any other. He set a royal diadem on her head and made her queen instead of Vashti.

"So," thought the scribe. "Now anyone can interpret as he will why the king fell in love with her. I'll just add something about the royal banquet and the tax remission in honor of the marriage." He drank his fruit juice and ate a few grapes. "Let me also remind the reader and listener of Esther's secret religion, because otherwise the story will not be as dramatic." He ate some flat bread stuffed with tangy goat cheese and pitted black olives carefully away from the writing table until he was finished. He gulped down the rest of the juice, and ordered the slave:

"Get me the Book of Chronicles! The one of King Ahashverosh!" When the slave rushed back with the scroll, the scribe rolled through it until he found what he was looking for, "Yes, this is the place to put Mordechai's discovery of the plot to kill the king. His deed is recorded right here."

As he completed the last line on the parchment, the chief scribe entered the room. Noting the Book of Chronicles on the table, he walked behind the younger man and read over his shoulder. The seated scribe sat quietly and awaited judgement.

"Yes," murmured the chief scribe, his belly almost on the head of the younger man. "Now go home and take tomorrow off. Go to the gardens with your wife and refresh yourself."

Delighted, the scribe bowed to his superior and happily walked home. "Yes," murmured the chief scribe again. "This is going very well."

Two days later, the scribe was back, ready to start the third chapter. It went easily for it merely involved describing the rise to power of Haman and his confrontation with Mordechai, who refused to bow low to him. Haman's rage was extended to all of Mordechai's people and he plotted to kill them all on a day decided upon by casting lots. Haman then manipulated the king into agreeing to his plot, first by accusing all Jews of treason, and second by promising to pay a huge sum of money for his agreement. The decree was issued, sealed with the king's signet, which the king had give to Haman to use as he saw fit.

When Mordechai learned of the decree he went into mourning, wearing sackcloth and ashes; this was imitated by all Jews in the empire. Esther alone seemed oblivious of the decree, and when it was reported to her that Mordechai was dressed in sackcloth, she had new clothing sent to him. Upon his refusal, Esther sent Hatakh, her personal slave who was also her most trusted servant, to learn what was going on. As a man, he could leave the women's quarters, but as a eunuch, he could also serve the queen with the king's trust.

Mordecahi had been awaiting Hatakh's arrival, knowing that whatever he told him would go directly to the queen and not be repeated to anyone else. In the palace environment of intrigue, danger lay on all sides. He told the eunuch of Haman's deeds and gave him a copy of the written text of the law passed declaring the destruction of the Jews. This written text, he hope, would impel Esther into action. Mordechai ordered the slave to show it to the queen and to charge her to go to the king to plead for her people. Hatakh did as requested.

"Now where are those pieces of parchment with the interviews with Hatakh?" the scribe said to his slave.

"Here they are, master. On the top of this pile of documents."

"Good, good. Peel me an orange while I copy this, and," he added with a smile, "peel one for yourself as well."

The queen replied: "All the king's courtiers and the people of the king's provinces know that if any person, man or woman, enters the king's presence in the inner court without having been summoned, there is but one law for him—that he be put to death. Only if the king extends the golden scepter to him may he live. Now I have not been summoned to visit the king for the last thirty days.

The next small piece of parchment contained Mordechai's reply, as memorized by Hatakh. *"Do not imagine that you, of all the Jews, will escape with your life by being in the king's palace. On the contrary, if you keep silent in this crisis, relief and deliverance will come to the Jews from another quarter, while you and your father's house will perish. And who knows, perhaps you have attained royal position for just such a crisis."*

The third piece of the interview with Hatakh contained Esther's response to Mordechai. *"Go, assemble all the Jews who live in Shushan, and fast on my behalf; do not eat or drink for three days, night or day. I and my young women will observe the same fast. Then I will go to the king, though it is contrary to the law; and if I am to perish, I shall perish!"*

The scribe showed his latest chapter to the chief scribe that afternoon.

"All right. You dealt with this issue through the interviews with the eunuch. Lucky for you he has such a prodigious memory. What will you do about the confrontations between the queen, the king, and Haman? You certainly cannot interview Haman, and the other two will not discuss the events with you."

"Well, some of the information was obtained by talking to the "invisible" people."

"Invisible? What do you mean?"

"The guards and unimportant slaves, like Haman's wife's slaves."

"How reliable are they?"

"A good point, sir. I've tried to corroborate one testimony with a second's. There really were very few secretive things. The only liberties I've taken have to do with Haman's emotions."

"As long as it is not with the queen's."

"Yes, sir."

On the third day, Esther put on royal apparel and stood in the inner court of the king's palace, facing the king's throne room; the king was seated on his throne facing the palace entrance. As soon as the king saw Queen Esther standing in the court, she won his favor, and he extended to Esther his golden scepter which he was holding. Esther neared and touched the tip of the scepter.

The king said to her: "What is it Queen Esther? What is your request? I would grant you up to half the kingdom."

Esther replied: "If it pleases Your Majesty, let Your Majesty and Haman come today to the feast that I have prepared for him."

The king said: "Tell Haman to hurry and do Esther's bidding."

So the king and Haman came to the feast that Esther had prepared.

At the wine feast, the king asked Esther: "What is your wish? It shall be granted. I would grant you up to half the kingdom."

Esther replied: "My wish, my request—if I have found favor in His Majesty's eyes and if it pleases Your Majesty to grant my wish and listen to my request—let the King and Haman come to the feast which I will make them; and tomorrow I will do as Your Majesty asks."

"All right, so you have the queen hesitating. You would too, in a situation like that," intoned the chief scribe. "She had fasted three days, had been terrified at the king's possible rejection of her appearance, and had organized a wine feast, all within a few hours of the king's positive reception."

"That is the point, sir. It also gave Haman the chance to reach both the peak of his elation—that only he and the king were invited to the feast—and the nadir of his evil because on the way home he saw

Mordechai again and in his rage, agreed to the proposal to hang him from a gallows fifty cubits high."

"That may have been the nadir of his evil, but it was not the nadir of his emotions, if I remember correctly."

"That is correct, sir. That is exactly what I am up to in chapter six."

"And whose testimony did you take for this?"

"The king's private attendants, of course."

"Of course."

"They saw the entire incident, sir."

"So they did. Continue, continue. You are more than halfway done."

That night, sleep deserted the king, and he ordered the Book of Records, the Chronicles, to be brought and read to him. And it was discovered that Mordechai had never been rewarded for saving the king's life. Just then Haman appeared, on his private vindictive mission to have the king agree to hang Mordechai. The king, on allowing him to enter his sleeping quarters, asked Haman: *"What should be done for a man whom the King desires to honor?"* Haman, in his hubris, said to himself, *"Who would the king desire to honor more than me?"* So he voiced his own fantasy: *"Let the royal garb which the king wore be brought, and a horse on which the king rode and on whose head a royal diadem has been placed. Let this attire and horse be put in the charge of one of the king's noble courtiers. Let the man whom the king desires to honor be dressed and paraded on the horse through the city's main street, while they proclaim before him: thus is done to the man whom the king desires to honor!"*

The king really liked this idea and ordered Haman: *"Quick, get the clothing and the horse as you said, and do this to Mordechai the Jew who sits at the king's gate. Omit nothing of all you have proposed."*

"Haman had no choice but to obey the king. Can you imagine his face? Can you imagine his feelings? I saw it myself and can attest to his fury," remarked the scribe to his helper.

"I did not see the parade, but I did see him when he returned to the palace courtyard, and then rushed off in humiliation," gleefully retorted the helper.

"Did you hate him too?" asked the scribe curiously.

"Not on a personal level, no. But it's not often that a prime minister gets to be publicly humiliated. And deservedly too."

"Yes, most deservedly," said the scribe softly. "But," the scribe went on in a louder voice, "before he could do anything, the royal escort arrived to bring Haman to the queen's feast. Imagine how this restored his sense of importance, marching behind the slaves in their bright outfits, walking down the long ornate corridors of the palace into the private royal quarters, decorated with the most luxurious wall hangings, mosaics and statues. The king was already seated at the low inlaid table on which were glazed bowls filled with the most perfect fruit, nuts, and candied seeds. Only when Haman was happily seated in this intimate setting, and the slaves had served the varied courses of the feast, constantly refilling the men's golden goblets with the best wines, did the king turn to the queen and repeat his question from the previous day: "What is your wish?"

He wrote for about half an hour, the only sound in the room was that of the rhythmic dipping of the quill into the pot of ink, and the scratching of the sharpened point on the smooth parchment.

Queen Esther replied: "If it pleases Your Majesty, my wish is that my life be granted to me and to my people. For we have been sold, I and my people, to be destroyed, massacred, and exterminated. Had we only been sold as slaves, I would have kept silent, for the adversary is not worthy of the king's trouble."

Thereupon King Ahashverosh demanded of Queen Esther: "Who is he and where is he who dared to do this?"

Esther replied: "The adversary and the enemy is this evil Haman!"

Haman cringed in terror before the king and queen. The king, in his fury, arose from the feast and went out to the garden, while Haman remained to plead for his life from Queen Esther, for he recognized that the king had decided to destroy him. When the king returned from the garden to the banquet room, Haman was lying prostrate across the low couch on which Esther reclined. The king cried: "Does he mean to ravish the king's wife?" Haman's face paled.

The scribe paused, thinking about whether the queen would approve his putting these words in her mouth. But the slaves he had questioned who had served the food and poured the wine and waved away the insects with the peacock feather fans had all repeated pretty much the same thing. They had also told him how terrified they had been, especially when the royal guards had suddenly appeared with their short swords draws. They had also heard Harvona, the eunuch, advise the king to hang Haman on the gallows that had been prepared by Haman for Mordechai. They had all watched open-mouthed as the guards had dragged a screaming Haman out, headed for the gallows.

He put away his work, leaving the latest parchment open, with small weights on the four corners, knowing that the chief scribe would read it in his absence. The scribe stood up and stretched, walked out of the palace and headed home. At supper that evening, which he and his wife ate on the small terrace overlooking the city of Shushan, he told his wife how far he had gotten in the writing of the scroll.

"That's it then, now that wicked Haman is dead," she exclaimed.

"No, not quite. There is still the edict of death for the Jews, sealed with the royal seal even though it was Haman who used it," he replied.

"I don't understand. If the king did not seal the edict, can't it be revoked?"

"No, for according to Persian law any edict written in the king's name and sealed with the king's signet may not be revoked."

"Did Queen Esther know this?"

"I am not sure. That is why I have to word the next chapter carefully, using the witnessed testimony in a way that covers all possibilities. The queen may or may not have set the king up to do what he did," said the scribe slowly as he thought things over. "Mordechai certainly is clever enough to have manipulated the situation…Well, he was desperate and therefore even if the king was manipulated, it doesn't matter in the long run." He finished his meal, drank his wine, and smiled at his wife.

"A few more days—maybe a week—and I will complete my task."

"Good. I can't stand the tension any more."

"Tension? What tension?"

Esther spoke to the king again, falling at his feet and weeping, and beseeching him to avert the evil plotted by Haman the Agagite against the Jews. The king extended his golden scepter to Esther and Esther arose and stood before the king. She said: "If it please Your Majesty and if I have found favor in Your Majesty's eyes and the proposal seems right to Your Majesty, and if I am pleasing—let dispatches be written counteracting those written by Haman son of Hamdata the Agagite which he wrote to annihilate the Jews in the empire. How can I bear to see the evil which will befall my people! How can I bear to see the destruction of my family!"

"A bit overdone," growled the chief scribe as he read it. "She may not approve."

"But I left out all the personal descriptions of how she gestured, her vocal intonations, her dramatic dress and makeup."

"True. You only put in what she in fact said."

"And she did make that long statement, the longest on record."

"I'll tell you what, my artistic writer/scribe/detective. I will let this stand and only show the queen the finished product. Perhaps when she sees the entire scroll, this long speech will be approved. Continue writing." He read the scroll one more time, then replaced it before the younger man.

"He mentioned nothing of manipulation," thought the scribe. "That means that I've succeeded in my presentation. Now I'll just starkly describe that the king hands his signet over to Mordechai, who has replaced Haman as minister to the king, to use as he saw fit."

"The first law could not be revoked, but Mordechai came up with a brilliant counter-plan. He had orders sent to all the Jews and the governors in the entire empire, sealed with the king's signet, that on the day that they were to be attacked, the Jews could assemble and fight back. The Jews were given permission not only to defend themselves but, should they be attacked, they could move from defensive to offensive and take plunder as well. This edict was carried by couriers riding on royal horses to the far reaches of the huge Persian empire, and publicly proclaimed everywhere," the scribe explained to his slave who was trimming more quills and filling the ink bowl."

"But being able to defend themselves was not a deterrent against attack."

"It was in part. It was also the knowledge that the new prime minister was Mordechai the Jew. He became more powerful with the passage of time, so the governors feared him."

"Were the Jews attacked on the thirteenth of Adar?"

"Yes, there were some who decided to try to attack the Jews, but the Jews were organized, armed, and inspired by Mordechai."

"Just Mordechai? What about Esther? Her role was just as important, if not more so," stated the slave heatedly.

This objection was stated also by his wife that evening. It set the scribe thinking on a new track. "Yes," he thought, "I now know how to conclude this scroll. I was going to end it with Mordechai's activities but not now."

The next day he described the fighting all over the Persian empire, the victory of the Jews, the hanging of Haman's ten sons and the extension of the fighting in Shushan by a day at Esther's request. He also described the celebration on the fourteenth of Adar by the victorious Jews, extended to the fifteenth to the Shushan Jews. He recorded Mordechai's dispatches to all the Jews to celebrate this day each year forever as a memorial to this victory, a day to be called Purim.

He showed his text to the chief scribe.

"So you have finished," he said.

"No sir. There are two points I would like to make which I cannot do openly." Seeing the hesitant look, the scribe added, "If you are worried, let me write the conclusion on a separate parchment and only if you approve will I put it into the main scroll."

"That sounds all right. I will return before sunset."

Then Queen Esther, daughter of Avihayil, wrote a second letter of Purim for the purpose of confirming with full authority the aforementioned one of Mordechai the Jew. Dispatches were sent to all the Jews in the hundred and twenty-seven provinces of the realm of Ahashverosh with an ordinance of equity and honesty: these days of Purim shall be observed at their proper time as Mordechai the Jew—and now Queen Esther—has obligated them to do.

And Esther's ordinance validating these observances of Purim was recorded in a scroll.

The slave watched the scribe sitting absolutely still. After some time had passed, he began to worry about his master.

"Sir," he whispered. "Sir," he said louder. The scribe blinked and picked up his quill one last time.

"No, it's not complete. I have to show not only that Esther was the main hero of the story, and that she was the power behind all the action, but also give an explanation for the lack of a formal record of her deeds. I cannot just write that women's actions were unimportant, but I can stress that the only actions that counted were those connected with the king and the ministers acting for him. Only public actions are recorded; women are part of private life."

The slave nodded his agreement.

King Ahashverosh imposed a tribute on the mainland and the islands.

"A very public act indeed, and one totally out of place in this scroll, unless the true meaning comes across," he thought.

All his mighty and powerful acts, and a full account of the greatness to which the king advanced Mordechai, are recorded the Annals of the Kings of Media and Persia.

"Go get the chief scribe," the scribe told his slave.

Within a few minutes the older man appeared. Without a word he was handed the draft text. The chief scribe read it over a few times before stating his opinion:

"She may not like it."

"Please, let me copy it over into the main scroll. If worse comes to worse, I will redo the entire last part on a new piece of parchment and sew it myself onto the rest of the scroll making sure it matches all the other parchment."

With a huge sigh, the chief scribe said: "You are most persuasive, young man. Copy it now, and I will present it to the queen tomorrow. She is anxious to see it."

"Yes sir. It will be done before I leave today."

Three days passed, three days of tension.

"Does she approve of my work? Does she understand why I wrote it as I did? What if she hates it, or parts of it?"

The scribe went to the scriptorium, overseeing the copying of the general scribes, correcting spelling and handwriting where needed. There was little talking, as each man concentrated on his task. They all knew of his nervousness and why. From down the long corridor, they all hear the approaching hurrying footsteps. The scribes gradually stopped writing and all heads turned to the archway.

"The queen approves the scroll!" proclaimed the chief scribe. "She compliments the compiler and," with a huge smile, "grants him whatever he wishes as a reward."

All eyes now turned to the young scribe.

"An audience," he burst out, "an audience with the queen. That's all I want."

"What? No gold? No jewels? No promotion?"

"An audience with Queen Esther," he stated again.

"I cannot promise it, for as you know, the queen does not usually enter the public part of the palace. But I will try."

The next day the scribe was informed that the queen would see him that afternoon, while the king was taking his nap. Sure enough, as the sun moved toward the west, the chief scribe appeared along with two guards to escort him through the maze of the palace to the small throne room just off the harem. With his heart beating in excitement, he followed the men, recognizing that they were getting close as the rooms were more and more richly decorated. The guards stopped at the entrance to a lavish room, and a eunuch stepped forward to announce the scribe's approach, preventing the chief scribe from going any farther.

The young scribe entered the room, and upon seeing the woman on the low throne, threw himself on the ground in a deep bow.

"Arise," a melodic feminine voice ordered. "Come closer. I wish to observe the intelligent and gifted young man who so cleverly wrote the scroll of Purim."

"Your Majesty, I am overwhelmed." And he was, for the queen was as beautiful as he had imagined, and with a voice like an angel. But as he dared to look in her eyes, his heart almost broke, for the queen's dark brown eyes were eyes filled with anguish.

"Oh, my Queen. I wrote as I did so that history would know of your heroism, of your…"

The queen said softly: "Of my…what?"

The scribe took a deep breath, and stepping as closely as he dared, switched from Persian in Hebrew.

"Of your sacrifice, my Queen. Of the pain at being cut off from your people, and at being married to a non-Jew."

"I had no choice. You hinted at it in your clever words."

"I worked very hard at that."

"Do you have any other words of comfort for me?"

"I had a dream. It was the same dream that I have been having since I started writing your scroll."

"Tell me of your dream, young scribe."

"I saw our people, a huge line of our people leading outward towards infinity. We were in exile all over the world, and we were crying. But then we read your scroll and were inspired. God has not left us in our exile, but works behind the scenes through people like you."

Esther's eyes filled with tears.

"My Queen, you will live forever in the Jewish people although you and your descendants are lost to us!"

"Thank you," she said, extending her hand. He bowed before her, and she motioned to a eunuch. "Give him his well deserved reward," she ordered in Persian. The eunuch handed to the scribe a small bag that clinked with coins.

"Come here," Esther said, and she removed a jeweled ring from her finger. "This is for you to remember me and," she added softly in Hebrew, "pray for me."

"I will name my firstborn girl after you," whispered the scribe, overwhelmed. He looked one last time into the eyes of the Queen, bowed low, and backed out of the room, to be escorted back to the scriptorium.

The scroll was there with a note attached to it. "To be added at the end of the text: *For Mordechai the Jew ranked next to King Ahashverosh and was highly regarded by the Jews and popular with the multitude of his brothers; he sought the good of his people and interceded for the welfare of them all.*

The note bore the seal of the prime minister.

Notes

The Biblical text for this chapter is The Scroll of Esther.

For background material, I recommend John H. Walton, *Ancient Israelite Literature in its Cultural Contest: A Survey of Parallels Between Biblical and Ancient Near Eastern Texts* (Zonderva, 1990); Robert Alter, *The Art of Biblical Narrative.* (Basic Books, 1981); William H. Stiebling, *Ancient Near Eastern History and Culture* (Routledge, 2016); Henri Stierlin, *Splendors of Ancient Persia* (White Star, 2006); Anna Vanzan and Catherine Bolton, *Ancient Persia: History and Treasures of an Ancient Civilization* (White Star, 2012).

Addendum

Reclaiming the Heroic Jewish Judith

One of the functions of biblical figures is to serve as role models. The narrative portions of the biblical texts are rich with information which can be understood on both a literal and a more historically complex level. Throughout the millennia of Jewish history, Bible commentators have provided us with a plethora of textual readings.

In analyzing female figures, however, one sometimes finds a disparity between what the text presents and how the commentators interpret them. Interestingly, this disparity manifests itself most blatantly in connection with the strongest women, namely Sara, Deborah, and Hulda.

In Genesis 18:9, when the three angels are visiting Abraham, they ask, "Where is Sara your wife? And he said: Behold in the tent (*ba-ohel*)." Rashi, living in France in 1040-1105 CE, is one of the most popular of all Jewish commentators. He explains that she was there because of modesty. That is certainly consistent with segregated roles in the ancient Middle East. But when the word *ohel* (tent) is used later to describe Jacob's location (Genesis 25:27), Rashi comments that he was in the "tent of Shem and Eber," meaning their houses of Torah study. Why use one explanation for Sara and another for Jacob? Could there be a gender discrepancy here?

More important than this interpretation is the destruction on the part of Rashi of the equal partnership of husband and wife, when he interprets Sarai's behavior with Hagar as one of selfishness and envy (Genesis 16:1-6). In interpreting Sarai's statement "My wrong be upon you," Rashi writes, "When you prayed to God you only referred to yourself as childless—you should have prayed for both of us and I too would have been remembered. Also, you wronged me by listening to what was said against me [by Hagar] and keeping silent." Why not see Sarai's actions in making her slave woman available to be a secondary wife, with the goal of adopting her child, as generous? In the women's later disagreements, Hagar, still a slave, acted improperly in the strictly demarcated roles of the ancient Middle East. Sarai could have punished her without consulting her husband, but diplomatically asked Abram, whereupon he told he what she already knew, namely that the women of the household came under the domain of the matriarch. Hagar's behavior demanded punishment, and the angel reminded her of this be calling out, "Hagar, Sarai's slave…"

More denigrating is the treatment of Deborah (Judges 4). Not only is Deborah's role diminished, but the commentators even claim that she was chosen by God only because of the good deeds of her husband, Lapidot. No, claim these men, Deborah never really "judged," because women cannot be judges. And even her prophecy—for she is labeled a prophet in the text—was wrong, because Sisera was delivered not into her hands but into Yael's. In other words, Deborah is punished for hubris. The ultimate act of denigration is the explanation of her name, *Devorah*, stating that it is not connected with the bee, that most useful and productive of insects, but with *dabbur*, the hornet, which only stings and produces nothing positive.

This attitude is carried over to the treatment of the prophet Hulda (II Kings 22:14-20), who lived in Jerusalem at the time of Jeremiah. She, too, is described as being chosen for prophecy due to the merits of her husband. She, too, is punished for hubris—in her case for referring to the king as "that man"—and she never has another prophecy. She, too, has the positive definition of her name changed into a negative one: *hulda* is a "cat", so important for catching rodents in the ancient Middle East, but this is changed into a "weasel", with all the negative connotations that this animal carries.

Two post-Biblical women are also treated in a denigrating manner by later commentators. The first is Salome Alexandra (139-67 BCE), the only queen of the Hasmonean dynasty, who, it was later said, never really ruled but merely followed the decision of her male advisors. After all, women could not have political power. The worst treatment of all was saved for Beruriah (second century CE), a scholar in her own right whose legal decisions are recorded in the Talmud. Medieval commentators describe a wager, a seduction, a suicide, and a flight. This was written a thousand years later, and is loosely based on an enigmatic phrase.

It seems that the scholars had made a decision, without actually calling a conference to discuss the issues. With the destruction of the Second Temple and the reality of the diaspora, the focus of the Jewish people was survival. Tools for survival included a community centered on a synagogue, education, and strictly defined roles for men and women. Men were leaders in the public and religious spheres, and women were wives and mothers, ostensibly leading the private sphere. Anyone who stepped out of line was brought back to reality through community action. Therefore, in a text-oriented religion, women who served as "bad" role models had their actions reinterpreted to suit the needs of the survival of a minority group.

So what could they do with an undeniably heroic female figure, named Judith, she who saved the Jews by beheading the enemy general and managing to escape with his head? The first step was to leave her out of the Tanakh. Esther, that scroll with so many *halakhic* issues in it, was included, but the tale of heroic Judith was not. Could it be that a passive Esther was preferable to an active and aggressive Judith? By placing the story of Judith in the *Apocrypha,* the "External Books," using the excuse that it is post-Prophetic or that there are *halakhic* problems with the text, the scholars were possibly hoping that it would disappear, just as they had hoped that the un-Jewish wedding ring would disappear, and therefore did not discuss it in the Talmud. Judith, too, was not discussed in the Talmud.

But the story of Judith did not disappear. It was referred to in Midrash literature, but more importantly, it was translated into Greek as part of the *Septuagint* project in Alexandria, whose scholars decided to include the *Apocrypha* books. With the rise of the Roman Republic, many Greek-speaking Jews from Alexandria moved to Rome. It may be presumed that they brought the *Septuagint* with them, and that copies were available in the *scuola* (synagogues) as well as in the homes of the very wealthy. The only other keepers of the *Septuagint*, as the Roman Empire turned Christian, were the monasteries.

A legitimate question that one could ask is how many Jews could actually read. The lower classes which initially formed the majority of the Jewish community in the Roman Republic probably could not read the Hebrew letters, since the tombstones that have survived from that time are carved with Greek words. They may have had a basic knowledge of the Greek alphabet and not been totally illiterate. It may be presumed that they learned by listening to texts being read aloud in the *scuola*. The synagogue as a community center for prayer, learning, and assembly was as old as the Second Temple period, and, if the language of the common people was Greek, many texts were probably read in that language. People had prodigious memories in those days, and it may be presumed that exciting narratives were preferred over dry points of law. There are few narratives more exciting than those of Judith and the Maccabees.

The small middle class presumably could read Hebrew, and some members of this group were educated enough to be able to read from the Torah on the Sabbath and to lead prayers. There was no scholarly class yet; that awaited the arrival of the slaves captured by Titus after the destruction of the Second Temple in 70 CE. In the aftermath of the destruction and the founding of the Academy (*Yeshiva*) in Yavneh, the connection between the Jews of Palestine and the Jews of Rome was strengthened.

But despite the growing control of the educated class of rabbis over the Jewish communities of Rome and southern Italy during the period of the Empire, Roman customs developed in an interesting direction. One markedly Roman custom is the reading of *Megillat Antiochus* in the synagogue during the holiday of Hanukah. Roman Jews also eat dairy foods on the holiday to commemorate the heroic story of Judith, who fed salty cheese to Holophernes to arouse his thirst, which would only be slaked by drinking large quantities of wine. They connect Judith's actions with the holiday of Hanukah, but do not mark it with the reading of the Book of Judith. Instead, the story has been reshaped and restructured into a religious poem entitled a *yotzer*, which is a kind of *piyyut*, or pious didactic expression in poetic form. The next question to be addressed is how far back the Judith poem can be traced. If it can only be traced back to the Renaissance, then its revival could be due to Judith's role in Christian Renaissance Italian creativity, which affected the Jewish attitude. If it was earlier than the Renaissance, the *yotzer* would be from a specifically Jewish context. The history of the *yotzer* as a poetic form has its origins in the religious poetry of the Torah, the earliest of which is the victory poem of Moses after crossing the Sea of Reeds. The next outstanding victory poem if that of Deborah after the Israelites defeated the Canaanites. Hymns to God were often composed during the Biblical period, and the most outstanding poet whose works survive was David, many of whose creations were collected in the Biblical book known as Psalms.

Poetry was the most popular art form in Middle Eastern general culture, and after the destruction of the Second Temple Jewish religious poetry took the form of the *piyyut*. *Piyyutim* are divided according to their liturgical purpose, differing in their history, structure, and distribution. One of the purposes of the early *piyyut* was to ensure variety in the obligatory prayers, and they were said mainly on Sabbaths and festivals. The oldest and anonymous poets did not use rhyme, instead stressing rhythm and style. One form of this early *piyyut* is the *yotzer*, which enjoyed great circulation in the period between the seventh and eleventh centuries. It is at this time that the Hebrew used moved from the lucid earlier style to a vague, exaggerated, and flowery style, which did not always follow Hebrew grammar; rhyme was the focus now, rather than rhythm. One of the most famous poets of this type of *piyyut* is Eleazar He-Kallir, whose religious paeans were composed in the most abstruse Hebrew, either to deliberately make the poem difficult to understand or to allow for multiple interpretations. The mystical nature of the text is trying to depict a level of the language that cannot be put into words; it is supposed to give the language a unique spiritual quality, something that is difficult to articulate in any language. This was the style of the earliest known European examples of the *yotzer*, which was written in southern Italy while it was under Byzantine control. It is to this part of Italy and to this period of time that the *yotzer* of Hanukah points, because it was a center of Jewish life in Italy at that time.

Tracing both the *yotzer* of Hanukah and the inclusion of *Megillat Antiochus* by Italian Jews is difficult, as very few manuscripts have survived from the ancient and early medieval periods. Yet, with the introduction of printing in Italy during the late Renaissance and the appearance of the prayer book in the form of either a *Mahzor* or a *Siddur*, research becomes more feasible. A search through the earliest extant examples of prayer books following Roman custom turns up both the *yotzer* of Hanukah, including the story of Judith and in many cases *Megillat Antiochus*, which is the story of the Maccabees. These did not come out of nowhere, but must have been part of a long tradition. The manuscripts of the early fourteenth-century prayer books that did survive attest to this.

Southern Italy was the confluence of two streams of Jewish intellectual life-that of Palestine and that of an earlier, specifically Roman tradition. The cities of Bari, Oria, and Otranto were *loci* of bustling Jewish communities which were at once part of the Greek-speaking Byzantine world and yet aware of what was going on in the world of Islam, which was spreading across North Africa into Spain in the west, and which was in control of the centers of Jewish religious creativity in the Academies of Baghdad. Closer to home, Sicily was invaded in 827 CE, and southern Italy was subject to attacks from then until 1061. Despite these conquests and reconquests, the Jews in southern Italy flourished.

In his medieval commentary on *Sefer Yetzira*, Shabtai Donnolo refers to books of Apocrypha, proving that Italian Jewish scholars read and studied these texts, including the Book of Judith. Book IV in the *Josippon* is a reworking of the *Book of Maccabees*, although it does not make reference to the story of Judith. This too supports the theory that there was a long continuous history of access to the various books of the Apocrypha and the Jews obviously did not need to use the Christian Bible to gain access to their own texts. No matter how open Italian Jews were to the larger culture, sacred texts were beyond the acceptable.

The author of the *yotzer* of Hanukah was Joseph ben Solomon (Yosef ben Shlomo). His name is worked into two acrostics, the first in the final few lines of the first stanza of the poem and second in the final few lines of the last stanza. It is accepted by scholars that he was from

Carcassonne, France, and that he lived before Rashi (1040-1105), who refers to this work in his commentary on Ezekiel 21:18. The Jews of the Rhineland originated in Italy, and the poetic styles of the two communities were similar, despite the fact that by the time of Rashi their Talmudic style diverged. We may thus presume that the author, although born in Carcassonne, traveled northward to the more Jewishly populous Rhineland and was either in touch with the southern Italian Jewish communities and their intellectual trends or himself traveled to these centers, something that was quite common then. His identification as "from Carcassonne" was a typical description, probably to differentiate him from other men with similar names. His knowledge of southern Italian poetic styles would also indicate the reverse: that the Jews of southern Italy knew of the poetic creations of the French Jews.

Why did the author use a *midrashic* variant for the Judith story instead of the Apocrypha version? Perhaps because *midrash* had an imprimatur of sanctity which the Apocrypha did not, and the creators of religious poetry therefore felt that it was more appropriate to use. But this reasoning only works for France, as in Italy the *Megillat Antiochus* is taken directly from the Apocrypha. Could it be that the Apocrypha narrative was too powerful for the author of the *yotzer*, for Judith is forcefully decapitating the general, and so he preferred the more toned-down versions? This would also fit with the fact that the author was French and not Italian, and French commentators like Rashi were already interpreting biblical texts in a manner that placed women in the preferred diaspora roles referred to above. Yosef ben Shlomo was, it seems, inspired enough by the story to use it in his poem, but only within the boundaries of *midrash*. The Italian Jews incorporated his *yotzer* into their Hanukah service along with their Apocrypha version of *Megillat Antiochus*. They were amenable to this because, as related above, they had a long tradition of connecting the Judith story to Hanukah and seemed to have no difficulty with strong women. They might not have liked the weaker *midrash* variant, but the poem was beautiful, and in the form of *piyyut* most admired at the time. The Italian Jews made up for the weaker Judith both in their manuscript illuminations and in the *hanukiyyot* that were crafted during the Renaissance, many of which depict Judith with her arms lifted in triumph above her head, holding the sword that was used to behead Holofernes.

The Italian Jews of the Renaissance may also have played another role, namely that of spreading the tale of the heroic Jewish Judith to other European Jews who came to northern Italy to have their books printed. The printing process took time, and these Jews stayed in local Jewish communities, hosted by the wealthier families there. They also went to Italian synagogues and witnessed—at Hanukah time—the Italian custom of reading *Megillat Antiochus* as well as the *yotzer*. It may be assumed that discussion of variations in customs ensued, with Italian Jews pulling volumes of the Apocrypha off their bookshelves to share their knowledge. This may well be how the first Yiddish version of the story began. There is no written proof of this method of transmission, but historians surmise it based on what is known. It would be wonderful to find a collection of sermons from that time which could serve as primary source proof. The art of the sermon already existed, and, again, the historian may justifiably surmise that the topic of the heroic Judith was a Hanukah favorite.

Unfortunately, neither the *Megilla* nor the *yotzer* is included in the latest Italian *Siddur*. As both Rabbi Elia Richetti of Venice and Rabbi Michele Ascoli of Rome noted, the service had become too long, and in the interest of "streamlining" certain things were dropped. Maybe Italian Jews feel no need for a figure like Judith any more, but that is not true for the rest of the Jews, for whom the story of the heroic Judith should be part of the school curriculum, discussed in sermons, and included in general knowledge.

Yotzer for Hanukah

> In praise of You because you retracted Your anger
> And You listened to my prayers, turning your anger against my enemy
> And making her like straw in a whirlwind;
> I remember and recall the past
> And the results of scarlet (acts)
> I will tell of the consequences and will not sleep;
> I will talk about the sufferings and the vendetta of Antiochus

Who killed my pious and butchered my priests,
When some idiotic people slandered me thus bringing destruction;
After that God gathered horses of fire
Upon which angels rode, angels with swords of fire
So that everybody in the Holy City would see the miracle.

Those arrogant idiots came to slander me
Because of this the king burned with rage
And decided to destroy those who multiplied in Goshen.
The king's rage grew suddenly bigger and bigger
This made me very afraid and threatened my life
I had to hide in the forest like an animal always prowling;
The king decided to destroy and crush the populace
He commanded his general Philippus
To force me to betray my faith and bow to the king's statue.

He ordered who would be made impure with pig
And whose foreskin cut out in a circular form
Whose corpses to throw down, refusing to save anyone;
He let live those who ate abominable idolatrous food
But disheartened those who stayed strong in their integrity
He broke and destroyed those who observed the laws of the Sages;
Two matrons who circumcised their sons
Were hanged by their breasts
And their babies were thrown with their mothers from the tower.

They thought of soiling Eleazar with their sacrifices
But he kept his faith and became even stronger
He rejected with contempt the orders of the cruel tyrant;
Who told him: "I cannot guarantee your life
Unless you will eat your holy meat while pretending to eat unholy meat
I will pretend to believe you so that I can free you."
He (Eleazar) answered crying: "I am ninety years old
And you are asking me to express my belief in God with a lie?
Stop talking to me for I will never change my life."

This righteous one did not betray his principles
And seeing that the old man chose to die rather than betray his faith,
The young men grew ever stronger;
Are You asking for a detailed account of the events
So You will burn with Your wrath the ram and the goat
Striking the head, the feet, the beard, and the neck?
Look and remember all the miseries

That have crippled and disgraced Your community
Will You abandon forever he who became so soiled?

I will now relate the story of the seven
Pious and believing brothers
Who were killed by the tyrant by fire;
Because they refused to eat from his sacrifice
They instead stayed true to He who created the world with His strength
The tyrant hacked apart the first with all his cruelty;
And into a bronze put full of boiling water
He put the hacked pieces of each limb
And skinned the head with his razor.

The tyrant in his hidden thought
Planned to slaughter his six brothers
Like lambs hanging from hooks;
He thought: I will seduce the seventh, the youngest.
"I will make you rich with gold" he drowsily said,
"And I decided to make you my viceroy."
But the youngest answered immediately.
He shouted: "Kill me, why are you hesitating?
I have no intention of bowing to other gods."

The cruel despot became even more enraged.
He kept hitting the innocent boy
Who grew stronger and enjoyed his suffering.
Their mother saw the sentence against her sons.
And she became so weak over her offspring
That her soul returned to her creator;
My will is so weak that I have not strength left.
Don't forget those pious people and their slaughter
Be gracious to those who merit it.

He who started all this made another stupid decision:
Those who will not rebel against my edict
And will follow Greek customs shall live;
But those who use their Hebrew names
Will be butchered, cut into pieces like a goat
Whose carcass is freshly hanging.
He made the ritual water impure
And the Pious ones separated from their wives
But God saw this great suffering and made a miracle.
The Lord who resides in Heaven

Made a source of ritual water for each
Because his pious ones bless him twice daily;
The tyrant then added another horror:
When the bride was to enter the house of her husband
She was first to sleep with the governor;
This was the last straw.
It lasted forty moons and four months,
Until Judah, the holy priest, rebelled.

When the glass was full, God gave charm
To the soon-to-be-married daughter of Yochanan the Hasmonean
Who gathered the people for the wedding feast;
The bride stripped off all of her clothing
And lifted a wineglass to the company
Who lowered their eyes so as not to look at her;
Her brother was in great rage against her
That the honored guests had seen this.
"How could you stand naked before them like a prostitute?"

To him the beautiful young woman replied:
"How dare you rebuke me so hypocritically
when you allow me to lie naked with an uncircumcised heathen?"
Then the spirit of God possessed Judah
And his heart was full of strength and courage.
He prayed and was possessed by an ardent zeal.
He gathered myrtle and spices
As was the custom to do for a wedding
In order to deceive the evil one, pretending to obey his law.

When the Greeks saw from afar the people singing and celebrating
Their leader said—"These important personages
Are finally willing to accept our customs";
He made his armed guards and servants go out
To usher in Matityahu and his sons.
Judah Maccabee drew on his strength;
With the ax used to cut wood he transfixed the adulterer.
He went after the enemy from Acco to Nemerim
Destroying it totally—this was told to Holofernes.

He gathered an army in order to subject Israel;
He encamped one mile off Zion.
My heart was agitated like the forest on the Carmel.
The people returned to their Creator

And everyone lamented, fasted, and cried.
And those more precious than gold meditated on the Torah.
A nobleman, Achior, prophesied to the king,
A nobleman and advisor to dukes and popes,
"They returned to the laws of the Torah and so they
                              will burn you in the oven."

When the demon heard this he went into a rage
And ordered that Achior be impaled
At the entrance of the main gate of the city.
He thought, "Tomorrow when I will burn the city
I will use my sword first on the head of that man
Because he said words in favor of my enemies."
But during that night, Judith came to my defense.
Her secret project was blessed and her reasoning excellent.
She encouraged her people and was a torch of fire against Greece.

Content that the city and its citizens were on the right path,
She was very happy and went with her slave,
And putting all of her hope in God
She stopped at the entrance of the enemy encampment
In order to undo their happiness and make them suffer
And feel the punishment for the sins of their leader.
They went to the king to laud her beauty.
"There is not one young woman like her in the entire province."
The king thus wanted to know her and sent for her.

He said: "Tell me where you come from."
She said: "I am from a family of prophets.
I can explain to you things that concern you, my king and master.
Suddenly tomorrow at this time,
Your arms will destroy the city like it was terracotta.
I came here to tell you this news without delay.
When you act within your anger,
Remember your servant
And the young men of my family who will serve in your house."

He whispered: "I will do anything you ask,
If you will do my will, I will elevate you in my house,
As well as elevate your father's family."
She replied: "I am not pure."
So he commanded to let her go, saying:
"Beware not to touch the young woman—she is going to purify herself."

He became like a horse in heat and started to dance.
He gave wine to all his soldiers and made a big party;
He became inebriated and so his neck became the object of a hunt.

Suddenly he fell profoundly asleep.
And his guests murmured that in order to violate the young woman
He lowered his head and is pretending to sleep.
They immediately left the tent, each going his way.
They rushed away from their king,
They hurried to their separate tents.
She, the clever one, prayed to God.
She cut off his head like a grain of wheat.
She took it and carried it back to raise the hopes of Israel.

They saw the head but did not believe her.
They ran to the man that he had wanted to impale in his rage
And he answered, "I swear that that is his head."
That night great were the manifestations of joy.
All the pain and sighs disappeared
Because in one moment the persecutor was erased
                              from the face of the earth.
They danced and celebrated all night
Praising the One who is terrible in his action
But protects his people with great mercy.

When the sun rose there was a great light in the morning.
They prayed to the Almighty and in the luminosity
Declared "Shma Yisrael!"
When the brigands heard the noise of the people,
They thought of awakening the king to prepare a trap,
But they saw him lying dead in his palace.
Their arrogance became humility and their courage dissipated.
They were afraid and pulled out their swords.
Their intended prisoners pursued them and cut them to pieces.

They killed them and made heaping piles of their bodies.
They sang hymns of thanksgiving.
The sages realized the great miracle that happened
And established reading the complete Hallel all eight days
And lighting specific lights each year, forever.
Today Shabbat and Hanukah coincide,
Praise to You from your nation, still delicate and tender,
And this nation will forever declare that the Kingdom belong to You.

> Your beloved people always search for You
> Because You did not stay silent,
> > they exalted You and declared You unique.
> Free them from their prison
> And they will all pay homage, O Holy One.

Reprinted from Sara Reguer, *The Most Tenacious of Minorities: The Jews of Italy* (Academic Studies Press: Boston, 2013), 155-167.

Bibliography

I. Primary sources—manuscripts

  A. Jewish Theological Seminary

    1. Mantua Mahzor, 1556-1560, 29b–33b.

    2. Mahzor Salonika, 1555-1556, 2-5.

  B. Palatina Library, Parma, Italy.

    3. Prayer book, Roman Rite, early 14th Century [1897], Folio 109a–110b.

    4. Prayer Book, Roman Rite, 14th Century [2221], 47b–48a.

    5. Prayer book, Roman Rite, late 14th Century [2578], 47a–56b.

    6. Prayer book, Roman Rite, second half 14th Century [2736], 25a–25b.

    7. Mahzor, Roman rite, 1390-1416 [350], 39b.

    8. Mahzor, Roman rite, 1462-3 [3141], 71a.

    9. Prayer book, Roman rite, 15th century[?]/14th century [1774], 92.

    10. Prayer book, Roman rite, 15th century [2573], 84.

    11. Prayer book, Roma rite, 15th Century [2576], 227b–229b.

II. Other sources

  1. Primary printed texts

    a. Ben-Gurion, Yosef. Yosipon. Jerusalem: Hominer, 1961 [Hebrew].

    b. Hartom, M. I., ed. Mahzor Minhag Italia. Rome, c. 1990.

c. Luzzatto, Shmuel David, ed. Mahzor. Livorno, 1866.

   d. Modena, Leone. Historia de riti Habraici. Venice, 1687.

2. Secondary sources

   a. Cohen-Mushlin, Aliza, ed. Jewish Art. Jerusalem: Magnes Press, 1987.

   b. Haberman, A. M. Toldot ha-Piyt ve-Hashira. Ramat Gan: Masada, 1972.

   c. Neuman, Abraham A. "Josippon: History and Pietism," Alexander Marx Jubilee Volume. New York: Jewish Theological Seminary of America, 1950.

   d. Roth, Cecil. The History of the Jews of Italy. Philadelphia: Jewish Publication Society of America, 1946.

III. Interviews

  1. Rabbi Elia Riccheti, Venice, January 26, 2008

  2. Rabbi Michael Ascoli, Rome, January 22, 2008

  3. Mr. Sandro Servi, Florence, January 20, 2008 (independent scholar)

  4. Dr. Piergabriele Mancuso, Venice, January 27, 2008.

www.ingramcontent.com/pod-product-compliance
Lightning Source LLC
Chambersburg PA
CBHW020331170426
43200CB00006B/342